FAQs for School Inspection

School inspections still have the potential to spread fear and panic through even the best-run schools, but this practical book will remove all of the anxiety, with its proven advice to help ensure a successful inspection.

Ideal for all teachers, whether newly qualified or with decades of experience, *FAQs for School Inspection* will guide the reader calmly through the pre- and post-inspection stages, offering valuable insights into what can happen during the inspection itself. Covering recent legislative changes and everything to do with school inspection, it outlines the teacher–inspector relationship and gives advice on coping with the potential stresses of inspections.

Organised into logical sections, the book covers issues such as:

- preparing for inspection
- being inspection-aware
- the effects inspection has on you personally
- what happens after inspection.

Complete with advice on using inspection to further personal and professional development, this ready-reference guide will allow teachers to play a confident and influential role in school inspection.

Elizabeth Holmes completed her PGCE at the Institute of Education, London. After teaching in London and Oxfordshire she became Head of History at a school in West Sussex. She now writes on education and health issues for a variety of national publications and websites, and prepares training and development materials. She has had many books published, including *The Newly Qualified Teacher's Handbook*, *FAQs for NQTs*, *Teacher Well-being* and *FAQs for TAs*.

www.elizabethholmes.info

FAQs for School Inspection

Practical advice and working solutions

Elizabeth Holmes

LONDON AND NEW YORK

First published 2009 by Routledge
2 Park Square, Milton Park, Abingdon, Oxon, OX14 4RN

Simultaneously published in the USA and Canada by Routledge
270 Madison Avenue, New York, NY 10016

Routledge is an imprint of the Taylor & Francis Group, an informa business

Typeset in Garamond and Gill by
Bookcraft Ltd, Stroud, Gloucestershire
Printed and bound in Great Britain by
CPI Antony Rowe, Chippenham, Wiltshire

British Library Cataloguing in Publication Data
A catalogue record for this book is available from the British Library

Library of Congress Cataloging in Publication Data
Holmes, Elizabeth, 1969–
FAQs for school inspection : practical advice and working solutions / Elizabeth Holmes.
p. cm.
1. School management and organization – Great Britain. I. Title.
LB2900.5.H65 2009
371.200941–dc22 2008025942

ISBN10: 0-415-43263-4 (hbk)
ISBN10: 0-415-33499-3 (pbk)

ISBN13: 978-0-415-43263-4 (hbk)
ISBN13: 978-0-415-33499-0 (pbk)

Contents

Author's note

At the time of writing, Ofsted is consulting on a range of proposals for changes to the system of inspection. In its quest to tailor inspections as closely as possible to the needs of schools, Ofsted is considering making the following changes to inspections:

- to inspect 'good' and 'outstanding' schools within six years, but to publish a 'health check' report between inspections;
- to inspect satisfactory or inadequate schools within three years;
- where improvements are needed, to make more frequent inspections;
- to make sure that schools know exactly what they need to do in order to become 'good' or 'outstanding' as well as the standards used for 'satisfactory' and 'inadequate';
- to take more account of the views of parents in deciding when a school might need inspection;
- to provide a letter for parents as well as pupils about the outcome of the inspection;
- to find out what teachers and non-teaching staff think of their school;
- to focus on the quality of teaching and learning as well as the school's ability to improve;
- to focus on whether the school provides good value for money.

As part of the consultation exercise, inspectors asked the following 15 questions (these were available as Annex A of the document *We Want Your Suggestions: New School Inspections from September 2009*, available from the Ofsted website: www.ofsted.gov.uk):

1. Is it appropriate to leave the inspection of good and outstanding schools for an interval of six years between inspections?
2. Are the proposals for what a 'health check' should include appropriate?
3. Are the proposals for targeting inspection at satisfactory and inadequate schools appropriate?
4. Is there a place for unannounced inspections?
5. Do you agree that we should put in place a national survey which captures the views of children and young people?
6. Do you agree that we should put in place a survey which captures the views of school staff?
7. Do you agree that a national survey of parents should take place annually?
8. Should the senior management of the school play a greater part in inspection by shadowing the inspectors?
9. Do you agree that inspectors should focus more attention on the achievement of different groups of pupils?
10. Do you agree that inspection should take more account of the capacity to improve?
11. Should Ofsted continue to use CVA as a measure of schools' progress?
12. Do you agree that we should define minimum standards for learners' outcomes?
13. Should we inspect the impact of partnerships on outcomes for pupils?
14. Should the inspectors' recommendations focus more precisely on the action the school should take to become good or better?
15. Should inspectors write a letter to parents setting out what the school should achieve by the next inspection and the actions the school needs to take to make that improvement?

The current plan is for new-style inspections to be implemented in September 2009.

Acknowledgements

Writing a book like this is impossible without the input of many people. During the course of my career in education to date, I've had the privilege of working with a large number of professionals as they prepare for and experience Ofsted inspection. Many of the questions they have posed have made their way into this book to serve as guidance and reassurance for others. I am very grateful to have been asked, and to have had the opportunity to answer, all such questions over the years. I'd also like to express my gratitude to Ofsted and its staff who have answered my many questions and offered insights, thoughts and considerations as well as the nitty gritty facts regarding Ofsted inspection. In addition, thanks must go to Philip Mudd and Alistair Shaw at Routledge, as well as the many people involved in getting this book into production, including Matthew Brown.

Finally, as ever, I would like to thank my family and friends whose unending support provides the backdrop against which my books are written.

Introduction

> What seem to us bitter trials are often blessings in disguise.
>
> Oscar Wilde

Inspection is an inevitable part of school life. From a child's first day at school to the day that he or she leaves full-time education, the current political agenda follows the view that educational achievement must be accounted for, and those at the frontline of this accountability, in the eyes of the ones with a responsibility to provide an educational service, are teachers.

The current system of inspection in this country, managed by the Office for Standards in Education, Children's Services and Skills (Ofsted) draws heavily in its inspections of schools on the National Curriculum and its associated tests (among other markers of attainment) in its assessment of the education being offered to the nation's children. This combination of inspection, delivery of the National Curriculum and National Curriculum tests (usually referred to as SATs) remains quite probably the most vehemently opposed development in education in recent decades, attracting the attention certainly of schools and their staff, but also of the media and the general public.

Yet of all these developments in education, it was the introduction of Ofsted inspections that seems to have caused, and continues to cause, the teaching profession unprecedented anxiety, and has elicited strong resistance. Even with the passing of time and the benefit of first-hand experience for many teachers and school leaders, combined with the fact that the notice period for inspection is relatively short, the anticipation of inspectors coming to visit *still* holds, for some, the worst of their fears of inadequacy, however adept and skilled they may be at their jobs.

Inspection has been a part of school life in one form or another since formal education began, and undoubtedly will continue to be central to education policy for the foreseeable future. As far as the Ofsted system of inspection is concerned, this book is not the place to discuss the merits or otherwise of its adopted methods. What this book sets out to do is to quell the fears, anxieties and concerns, and answer all the typical questions that teachers have about the prospect of inspection. It also seeks to highlight the extent of the manoeuvrability that teachers have within this system of inspection and help to maximise the potential for gaining both personally and professionally from inspection. With correct information (rather than folklore and rumour!) and on-going effective preparation, it is possible to lessen any potential negative impact that inspection may have and maximise the benefits. By acknowledging this, inspection is seen less as an inevitable hurdle in school life and more as a valuable tool in the development of both the school and the individual teacher.

The direction that this book took was heavily dependent on the questions and concerns of the many teachers and headteachers that I consulted. It also draws on the questions that inspectors themselves have been asked about the process of inspection. All these questions, anecdotes, testimonies, ideas and coping mechanisms from many corners of educational life have found their way in here to support *your* experience of inspection. In many cases the advice included has been tested over time and chosen specifically to encourage you to face inspection squarely and with energy, rather than resignation.

There are enormous difficulties in offering a path through inspection as we know it today. An inspection forces many teachers outside their comfort zones: zones that are already extraordinarily far-reaching. By laying bare the flesh and bones of inspection via the common concerns and anxieties of teachers today it is hoped that this book will enable you to expand your comfort zone to include and even to embrace regular inspection. That said, significant differences exist between schools regarding the way in which inspections are anticipated. For this reason, sources of external support for teachers have also been indicated where possible.

Research for this book has evoked diverse remarks about inspection from those involved in education. I write as someone who has experienced many hours of observation in inspection as a teacher and who has also been through inspection from another perspective as a school governor. While I ultimately enjoyed the opportunities that inspection gave me to focus on my work as a teacher and contribution as a governor, I have been mindful of the fact that not all teachers feel the same way. For some, inspection holds a cocktail of fear, insecurity, anxiety and apprehension; and for a few, this is thought to have contributed to the most tragic of outcomes.

We are all very different from each other in our perceptions, our strengths and our aptitudes, so there can be no magic 'fix' to suit all for the professional anxieties we may face. If you would like to contribute your thoughts on how inspection can best be experienced positively, you can email me at: eh@elizabethholmes.info.

As you will appreciate, nothing remains static in education and inspections themselves have changed over the years. They have been tweaked and developed so that the chances are each time you experience inspection it will undoubtedly be different to some extent from the previous occasion. At the time of writing, a consultation on improving the inspection of schools has been announced and more changes are imminent. These have been incorporated where possible and sources of further information provided. Regardless, there are many basic principles of inspection which are covered here and which will remain the same: how you cope with the whole concept of inspection, how you might be better prepared for it, how to thrive throughout it and how to reflect to make the most of it, to name a few!

While not everything can work for everyone, the ideas in this book will, I hope, help you to thrive rather than survive during your inspection. Better still, may they inspire in you positive and creative solutions and responses to whatever inspection has in store for you. Good luck!

Note

Any advice given in this book concerning the health and well-being of readers is for information and guidance only and is not intended to replace the advice of a qualified healthcare practitioner. Symptoms of stress, in particular, require extremely careful management, and while self-treatment can help tremendously, it is always wise to have such symptoms registered with your chosen healthcare provider. Neither the author nor the publisher can be held responsible for any consequences that occur as a result of following the guidance contained herein.

A word about the scope of this book

Ofsted is now responsible for inspecting and regulating a wide range of services. These responsibilities include:

- the inspection of adult learning and training which used to be undertaken by the Adult Learning Inspectorate;
- the regulation and inspection of children's social care which used to be undertaken by the Commission for Social Care Inspection;
- the inspection of the Children and Family Court Advisory and Support Service (CAFCASS) which used to be undertaken by Her Majesty's Inspectorate of Court Administration;
- the registration and inspection of childcare as well as arrangements for social care and support of children and young people;
- the inspection of all maintained and some independent schools;
- the inspection of further education, all publicly funded adult education and training and some privately funded training provision;
- the inspection of initial teacher training.

This book, however, focuses on the experiences of teachers undergoing inspection in mainstream maintained schools. You can find out more about inspection in other settings from the Ofsted website: www.ofsted.gov.uk.

CHAPTER 1

Introduction to Ofsted

> The first and most important step toward success is the feeling that we can succeed.
>
> Nelson Boswell

Introduction

School inspection in England is all about Ofsted. As an organisation it's fair to say that it has had a bit of an image issue. Its popularity over the years hasn't been that great and many schools and their staff would probably rather that it didn't exist at all. But Ofsted has grown and developed, just like the many schools it has inspected over the years, and is here to stay. Knowing a little about its background, the way that it operates and the context in which it carries out its responsibilities can help greatly in your preparations and on-going readiness for inspection. Knowledge is power, and this is just the kind of background information that helps to nurture familiarity with what is essentially a potential development tool for you and your school.

This chapter explores the following ideas:

- the meaning of Ofsted
- what Ofsted is
- what Ofsted does
- how Ofsted is structured
- where Ofsted operates from
- HMCI roles and responsibilities

- Ofsted's users, providers and stakeholders
- types of Ofsted inspector
- inspecting Ofsted
- general standards for public office
- Ofsted's vision
- the departmental and annual reports
- school inspection around the UK
- changes in Ofsted
- developing proposals for change
- reasons for change
- ordering Ofsted publications.

What does 'Ofsted' actually stand for?

Ofsted stands for the Office for Standards in Education, Children's Services and Skills. Prior to 2007, Ofsted stood for the Office for Standards in Education.

What is Ofsted?

Ofsted, as we know it today (in other words, the Office for Standards in Education, Children's Services and Skills rather than the Office for Standards in Education), is a non-ministerial government department and an independent regulator. This latest incarnation was created on 1 April 2007 from a merger between the old Office for Standards in Education and the Adult Learning Inspectorate. Today's Ofsted builds on four previous inspectorates. In short, Ofsted provides the country with information on the quality of the public services it is concerned with.

What does Ofsted do?

Ofsted, today, is responsible for all the regulatory and other inspection activities that the former Ofsted was responsible for but it also has additional responsibilities as outlined here:

- the inspection of adult learning and training which used to be undertaken by the Adult Learning Inspectorate;
- the regulation and inspection of children's social care which used to be undertaken by the Commission for Social Care Inspection;
- the inspection of the Children and Family Court Advisory and Support Service (CAFCASS) which used to be undertaken by Her Majesty's Inspectorate of Court Administration;
- the registration and inspection of childcare as well as arrangements for social care and support of children and young people;
- the inspection of all maintained and some independent schools;
- the inspection of further education, all publicly funded adult education and training and some privately funded training provision;
- the inspection of initial teacher training.

As a result of the Education and Inspections Act 2006 the 'new' Ofsted is charged with promoting improvements in the public services that it inspects and regulates. It has to ensure that all of these services focus on the interests of children, parents, learners and employers and that they are both efficient and effective.

How is Ofsted structured?

There are currently two features to the leadership of Ofsted: a Corporate Management Team and a non-executive Board. The Corporate Management Team has a duty to ensure the effective corporate and strategic management of Ofsted. It is led by HMCI who is supported by the Directors of five divisions:

- Children
- Learning and Skills
- Education
- Corporate Services
- Finance.

There is an Ofsted Board which was established as a result of the Education and Inspections Act 2006 in order to provide strategic direction and oversight of Ofsted. It is a non-executive Board with ten members including the Chairman and HMCI. Board members are appointed by the Secretary of State for Children, Schools and Families and they are appointed on merit and not on political activity. The Board meets four times a year and is responsible for engaging directly with users of the Ofsted service, with a duty to have regard to their views. It also has a statutory purpose in encouraging improvement as well as responsibilities for corporate governance so that Ofsted performs its duties effectively and efficiently.

In performing its duties, the Board has to have regard to the following:

- the need for the rights and welfare of children to be promoted and safeguarded;
- the views and satisfaction levels of the children, parents and employers that it is serving;
- the need for Ofsted inspection to be proportionate (this applies to its regulatory actions too);
- developments in approaches to inspection;
- best practice.

You can access schedules of future Board meetings as well as minutes and papers for meetings which have taken place via the Ofsted website (see below). If you are interested in finding out more about how Ofsted is run, you can download Ofsted's *Corporate Governance Framework* from the Ofsted website (see below).

Where does Ofsted operate from?

The London office of Ofsted is in Kingsway, Holborn, in central London. Contact details are as follows:

London	Alexandra House 33 Kingsway London WC2B 6SE
North Regional Centre	Royal Exchange Buildings St Ann's Square Manchester M2 7LA

Midlands Regional Centre	Building C Cumberland Place Park Row Nottingham NG1 6HJ
South Regional Centre	Freshford House Redcliffe Way Bristol BS1 6NL

Postal communication should be sent to the Manchester office. You can email Ofsted via: enquiries@ofsted.gov.uk Telephone numbers are as follows (lines are open from 08.00 to 20.00 Monday to Friday):

- 08456 404045: information about education, adult skills or local authority children's services;
- 08456 404040: information about any other aspect of Ofsted's work;
- 0161 618 8524: for Minicom users.

Who is Her Majesty's Chief Inspector of Schools in England and what are the responsibilities of the role?

At the time of writing, Her Majesty's Chief Inspector of Schools in England (HMCI) is Christine Gilbert. Interestingly, the office of HMCI dates right back to the mid-nineteenth century. It was the 1992 Education Act which saw it being re-established though.

The roles and responsibilities of HMCI are varied and include the following:

- Inspection and regulation of services within his or her remit.
- The overall organisation, management and staffing of Ofsted and its procedures in financial and other matters, including conduct and discipline.
- Being the Accounting Officer of Ofsted, and answerable to Parliament for ensuring that all the resources available are used as they should be. HMCI is also responsible for ensuring value for money.

- Keeping the Secretary of State for Children, Schools and Families fully informed about the quality of the activities that HMCI must be involved in and the standards achieved by those for whose benefit these activities are carried out; improvements in the quality of the activities and standards; the extent to which these activities are user-focused; the effective and efficient use of resources.
- If the Secretary of State for Children, Schools and Families requests information or advice on anything within the remit of HMCI, this must be given. Similarly, HMCI may give advice in connection with any of the activities in his or her remit at any time.
- Other functions may be assigned to HMCI by the Secretary of State.

Ofsted's Corporate Governance Framework (June 2008) explains that HMCI also has a duty to perform his or her functions to encourage:

- improvement in the activities within HMCI's remit;
- carrying out such activities as user-focused activities;
- the efficient and effective use of resources through the carrying out of these activities.

You can find out much more about the finer details of HMCI's duties and responsibilities from the Ofsted website (see below).

I've heard people refer to Ofsted's users, providers and stakeholders. What are these categories?

Users are those who benefit in some way, either directly or indirectly, from the services that Ofsted has responsibilities for inspecting or regulating. In other words, users are children and young people, parents and carers, adult learners and employers. Providers are all those who provide the services that are inspected or regulated by Ofsted. These are schools, colleges and childcare providers; children's homes and fostering and adoption services; adult, community, work-based and other learning services (including Learndirect and NextStep); secure estate and judicial services; and local authorities. Other stakeholders are Ofsted's contracted partners; other inspection and regulatory bodies; government departments and agencies; governors; stakeholders who comment on or scrutinise Ofsted's services and/or benefit from its success; local, national and European politicians; press and media; and the wider general public.

How many types of inspector are there?

There are two types of inspectors for schools:

- Her Majesty's Inspectors (HMI), who work directly for Ofsted;
- Additional Inspectors (AI), who are employed by Ofsted's regional inspection service providers (RISPs). RISPs are responsible for recruiting and training AIs but this has to be to the standards specified by Ofsted.

You can find out more about the organisations – which include Nord Anglia Education, the Centre for British Teachers, the Prospects Group and Tribal Group – that work in partnership with Ofsted to provide school inspections from the Ofsted website (see below).

If you are so inclined, you can take a look at the full list of additional inspectors of schools, further education colleges and independent schools. As Ofsted explains:

> Under schedule 1, paragraph 2 (6) of the Education Act 2005, HMCI is required to publish the names of those persons who are notified to him [or her] by an inspection service provider as persons with whom the inspection service provider proposes to make arrangements for carrying out of inspections on behalf of HMCI.

You can find this list on the Ofsted website (see below).

Who inspects Ofsted?

The Ofsted Board has responsibilities to monitor information it receives about Ofsted's performance and to ensure that it carries out all of its duties and functions as effectively and efficiently as possible. It really has to oversee what goes on at Ofsted to make sure that strategic objectives and targets are met and that its use of resources amounts to value for money. The Board also encourages corporate social responsibility and openness about the work of the organisation. This might seem as though Ofsted is both judge and jury from within, but Board members do have to abide by a Code of Conduct which covers public service values, the responsibilities of individual Board members, personal liability and the process used for investigations.

There are other features of accountability which apply to Ofsted including external audits and value for money examinations, the departmental report and the annual report (see below).

You can find the Code of Conduct for Ofsted Board members in Annex A of Ofsted's *Corporate Governance Framework*, available as a free download from the Ofsted website (see below).

In addition, Ofsted gives schools quality assurances, and the Ofsted website contains documents about this.

Are there any general standards that people who hold public office should abide by?

Yes, there are. They are known as the Seven Principles of Public Life and they have been set out by the Committee on Standards in Public Life. You can find out all about these principles on the Committee on Standards in Public Life website (see below). The principles are as follow:

The Seven Principles of Public Life

Selflessness
Holders of public office should take decisions solely in terms of the public interest. They should not do so in order to gain financial or other material benefits for themselves, their family, or their friends.

Integrity
Holders of public office should not place themselves under any financial or other obligation to outside individuals or organisations that might influence them in the performance of their official duties.

Objectivity
In carrying out public business, including making public appointments, awarding contracts, or recommending individuals for rewards and benefits, holders of public office should make choices on merit.

Accountability
Holders of public office are accountable for their decisions and actions to the public and must submit themselves to whatever scrutiny is appropriate to their office.

Openness
Holders of public office should be as open as possible about all the decisions and actions that they take. They should give reasons for their decisions and restrict information only when the wider public interest clearly demands.

Honesty
Holders of public office have a duty to declare any private interests that relate to their public duties and to take steps to resolve any conflicts arising in a way that protects the public interest.

Leadership
Holders of public office should promote and support these principles by leadership and example.

There are also Nine Principles of Public Service Delivery which were originally derived from Service First, the UK Cabinet Office.

Nine Principles of Public Service Delivery

Every public service should:

Set standards of service
Set clear standards of service that users can expect; monitor and review performance; and publish the results, following independent validation wherever possible

BOX CONTINUES OVERLEAF

Be open and provide full information
Be open and communicate clearly and effectively in plain language, to help people using public services; and provide full information about services, their cost and how well they perform

Consult and involve
Consult and involve present and potential users of public services, as well as those who work in them; and use their views to improve the service provided

Encourage access and the promotion of choice
Make services easily available to everyone who needs them, including using technology to the full, and offering choice wherever possible

Treat all fairly
Treat all people fairly; respect their privacy and dignity; be helpful and courteous; and pay particular attention to those with special needs

Put things right when they go wrong
Put things right quickly and effectively; learn from complaints; and have a clear, well publicised, and easy-to-use complaints procedure, with independent review wherever possible

Use resources effectively
Use resources effectively to provide best value for taxpayers and users

Innovate and improve
Always look for ways to improve the services and facilities offered

Work with other providers
Work with other providers to ensure that services are simple to use, effective and co-ordinated, and deliver a better service to the user.

Does Ofsted itself have any guiding principles?

Ofsted has a vision as follows:

Ofsted's vision

We inspect and regulate:

> to achieve excellence in the care of children and young people, and in education and skills for learners of all ages.

The Office for Standards in Education, Children's Services and Skills came into being on 1 April 2007. The new organisation brings together the wide experience of four inspectorates in order to make a greater difference for every child, and for all young people and adult learners. With parents and employers, these are the key users of the services we inspect and regulate. We shall listen to what they tell us. Their educational, economic and social well-being will promote the success of England as a country.

We shall communicate our findings from regulatory visits and inspection to those who have an interest in our work, including providers of care, education and training; administrators and policy-makers. In doing so, we aim to improve current provision and outcomes, to raise aspirations and to contribute to a longer term vision for achieving ambitious standards.

We report impartially, without fear or favour, demonstrating integrity in all we do. But we work closely with partners and stakeholders, including government departments and other agencies, to make sure that our inspection and regulation are used to realise our vision.

To contribute to improving services and their outcomes for users we will report with impartiality and integrity. We will communicate our findings with, and listen to, all who have an interest in improving them, from service providers to policy-makers. We want to raise aspirations and contribute to a longer term vision for achieving ambitious standards.

Reference: www.ofsted.gov.uk

What are the departmental report and the annual report?

The departmental report is produced by HMCI each year and it reviews the work of Ofsted for that year. It also looks at the way in which Ofsted has contributed to the improvement of the services within its remit. This report has to be laid before Parliament by the Secretary of State for Children, Schools and Families.

The annual report also has to be laid before Parliament by the Secretary of State. This report details the state of the services within Ofsted's remit and it draws on the inspection data relating to inspections undertaken that year.

What is Her Majesty's Chief Inspector's annual report for?

Every year, HMCI reports to Parliament on the quality and standards of education in England. This report is based on all the inspections which were conducted by Her Majesty's Inspectors and Additional Inspectors throughout the course of the previous academic year. It is also based on inspections which have a specific themed focus. Ofsted describes this as a 'state of the nation' report and aims for it to ensure that inspection drives improvement not only in education policies but also in individual schools.

Is it only England that has a system of school inspection?

No, school inspection takes place in all the countries of the UK. In Wales, the inspection of schools is the responsibility of Estyn: Arolygiaeth Ei Mawrhydi dros Addysg a Hyfforddiant yng Nghymru (Her Majesty's Inspectorate for Education and Training in Wales). It inspects: early-years provision in the non-maintained sector; primary schools; secondary schools; special schools; pupil referral units; independent schools; further education; youth support services; local education authorities; teacher education and training; work-based learning; Careers Wales companies; the education, guidance and training elements of the

New Deal; and adult community-based learning. It also provides advice to the Welsh Assembly Government on a range of matters linked to education and training.

In Scotland, HM Inspectorate of Education (HMIE) has responsibilities for school inspection. It is an executive agency of the Scottish Government and its inspectors review, inspect and report on education provision in: primary, secondary and special schools; further education institutions (under contract to the Scottish Further and Higher Education Funding Council); initial teacher education; community learning and development; care and welfare of pupils; the education functions of local authorities; prison education; and children's services, as well as in other contexts as necessary.

Inspection in Northern Ireland is the responsibility of the Education and Training Inspectorate. It provides inspection services for the Department of Education Northern Ireland (DENI), the Department for Employment and Learning and the Department of Culture, Arts and Leisure. At the time of writing, schools are inspected once every five to seven years. The inspectorate also provides evidence-based advice to ministers and departments to assist in the formulation and evaluation of policies in education, training and youth.

You can find out more about the comparative education systems of each of the four countries of the United Kingdom in *Whitaker's Almanack* (see below).

Does Ofsted ever change over time?

Yes, Ofsted has undergone some quite considerable changes over the years since it came into being and even the post-2007 Ofsted is about to undergo more change. In May 2008, Her Majesty's Chief Inspector announced a major consultation on proposed changes to the system of school inspection. This consultation is detailed in the document *A Focus on Improvement: Proposals for Maintained School Inspections from September 2009* available from the Ofsted website (see below).

There are some key differences between the current arrangements and the new proposals (as listed in the above-mentioned document):

- Inspections will be more tailored to the needs of the school. All schools judged to be satisfactory or inadequate in their most recent full inspection will be inspected within three years; in general, schools judged good or outstanding will be inspected within six years, although one 'health check' report will be published in the intervening years.
- Inspectors will take more account of the views of parents in deciding when a school needs to be inspected.
- There will be increased focus on the progress made by different groups of children and young people which could include those most likely to underachieve, the most vulnerable and the most able. The well-being of learners, the quality of learning and the quality of teaching will feature strongly in the inspection.
- Inspectors will take more account of the capacity of the school to improve than in the current arrangements.
- Schools' senior managers will be involved more consistently in the inspection process.
- The inspection of federations and partnerships will be coordinated.
- Some inspections will have a specific focus, such as looked after children. Criteria for outstanding and good schools will be more explicit and standards for satisfactory and inadequate will be defined so that schools are much clearer about what they need to do to improve.
- Ofsted will report more explicitly on whether the school provides good value for money.
- Ofsted will explore whether 'no notice' inspection is feasible.

For more on the consultation and the document *A Focus on Improvement: Proposals for Maintained School Inspections from September 2009* take a look at the Ofsted website (see below).

Who is it who develops proposals for change in the way in which Ofsted operates?

Ofsted consults headteachers and other professionals as well as holding discussions with parents, children, teachers, governing bodies, local authorities and other stakeholders in the process. Ideas are gathered and used to inform the proposals that Ofsted puts forward. The next stage is for these proposals to be tested and developed further through a series of pilot studies involving local authorities, schools, parents and pupils. These pilots are then evaluated and the outcomes will be disseminated.

Why does Ofsted want to change school inspection? Does that mean it isn't working at the moment?

No, that's not what Ofsted feels at all. The rigours of inspection mean that schools necessarily develop over time in their response to Ofsted's requirements. This means that the system of inspection needs to be developed in order to take account of schools' ever-growing skills of self-evaluation. Ofsted also has targets to improve the service it provides which means that change over time is inevitable.

Another dimension to this need to develop the system of inspection is that in comparison with international standards, education in England has apparently 'stalled'. Naturally inspection is one thread of the overall progress plan and so it must adapt to new targets and agendas. There are also big concerns about the gaps which have been developing between attainment achieved by particular groups of children. The Children's Plan has also set ambitious targets for schools and the country as a whole to strive for, and all of this feeds into the need for Ofsted to deliver according to the needs of children and young people of the twenty-first century.

It isn't all about improvement either. Those schools which are doing well consistently require slightly different inspection timescales than schools which have a little more progress to make. Allowing for these variations can help schools to do what they do best and Ofsted to do what it does best. Ofsted has also highlighted the need to help schools to move from 'good' to 'outstanding' and prevent slippage from 'good' to 'satisfactory'. It is hoped that a revised system of inspection will be better able to help facilitate this. Interestingly, 20 per cent of schools inspected since 2006 have received the so-called 'light touch' inspections and in April 2007 this was increased to 30 per cent on a trial basis. The growing body of information that Ofsted has accumulated on schools is making it increasingly possible for inspectors to identify accurately which schools would benefit from the light touch approach. All of this experience can, and will, feed into the proposed changes.

How can I order Ofsted publications?

There are Ofsted publications on every feature of the organisation's work which might prove useful to you. Whether you are interested in guidance, research or reports, it's all available, most of it free of charge, downloadable from the Ofsted website (see below). A small number of publications are also available in printed format. These can be ordered from the Ofsted publications centre via freepublications@ofsted.gov.uk or by ringing 07002 637833 or faxing 07002 693274.

You might also be interested in subscribing to the Ofsted e-newsletter and email alerts. This all helps in your general preparedness for inspection! If you are interested, take a look at the 'Subscribe' section of the Ofsted website (see below).

Find out more ...

- The Ofsted website can be accessed here: www.ofsted.gov.uk
- *Whitaker's Almanack* is available in any reference library or good bookshop. Find out more from the website: www.whitakersalmanack.co.uk
- The website for the Committee on Standards in Public Life can be accessed via: www.public-standards.gov.uk

CHAPTER 2

All about school inspection

> An inconvenience is an adventure wrongly considered.
>
> Gilbert K. Chesterton

Introduction

As we have seen, Ofsted now has a very wide range of responsibilities of which the inspection of schools is just one. While there are no tricks whatsoever in this system of inspection, it is helpful to know what to expect and to become familiar with the language and landscape of school inspection. Naturally, the best source of factual information on the nitty gritty of inspection comes from Ofsted itself and its website carries all the relevant documents you may need as a teacher about to experience inspection. That said, there remains a need for teacher-to-teacher communication about school inspection, to share knowledge and 'demystify' any remnants of uncertainty that may still remain. After all, life in schools is incredibly hectic and staying on top of everything *all* the time is practically impossible!

This chapter explores ideas around:

- why we have school inspection
- inspection and the law
- what schools are inspected
- inspection and faith schools

- inspection and specialist schools
- the main features of school inspection
- the frequency of school inspection
- the duration of school inspection
- HMI and inspection
- 'reduced tariff' inspections
- the notice period for inspections
- deferring inspections
- the inspection of subjects
- paperwork
- the Ofsted grades defined
- the 'special measures' category
- the 'notice to improve' category
- the inspection of new schools
- the code of conduct for inspectors
- the involvement of parents in inspections
- reasons for publishing inspection reports
- availability of Ofsted reports
- RAISEonline
- the self-evaluation form – SEF
- the inspection of leadership and management
- the common inspection schedule for schools and other post-16 provision
- what inspectors evaluate
- the Every Child Matters agenda
- what Ofsted reports on
- the basic questions that Ofsted looks at during an inspection
- how inspectors spend their time in schools
- accountability
- what inspection isn't about
- the Pre-Inspection Briefing (PIB)
- gathering evidence
- what goes into the written report
- inspectors' communication with pupils
- the concept of value for money
- inspection of schools outside England

- quality assurance of inspections
- the complaints procedure
- possible outcomes.

Surely schools should be left to get on with their work and not have to worry about inspectors coming in to see what they are doing. Why do we have school inspection?

The reasoning behind having school inspection (and remember, we have had one form or other of school inspection virtually since education began) is that it provides an independent and external view of the most important features of school life: quality and standards. The main impetus behind inspection is to raise standards and consequently the well-being of children and young people. The hope is that this will then feed into improvements in their overall quality of life. That's the aim, anyway! Evidence both from Ofsted and from independent research does show that there is tangible benefit to be had from the regular monitoring of schools, so while inspection is shown to help towards raising standards, it will be here to stay.

Is there a law which decrees that school inspection should take place?

Afraid so! School inspection is carried out under Section 5 of the Education Act 2005. There are also inspections which take place under Section 8 of the Education Act 2005. This gives HMCI the powers to inspect any school. Monitoring visits to schools are undertaken under Section 8 of the Act, even though inspectors use the guidance that applies to Section 5 inspections. And if you really want to get confused by it all, HMCI can treat Section 8 inspections as Section 5 inspections under Section 9 of the Act. Got it?

Monitoring inspections, both for schools causing concern and for schools that are not deemed to be a cause for concern, are different from Section 5 inspections. Your headteacher will be able to tell you what kind of inspection your school undergoes. You can find out more about this from the Ofsted website (see below).

What schools are inspected?

The legislation on inspection covers all maintained schools and some non-maintained schools.

My school is a faith school – does it still have to be inspected?

Yes, but there are some subtle differences, which are detailed here. The *Framework for Inspecting Schools in England from September 2005*, April 2008 edition, states that:

> Some schools are designated under Section 69(3) of the School Standards and Framework Act 1998 by the Secretary of State as having a religious character. The content of collective worship is not included in the Section 5 inspections of such schools, but under Section 48 of the Education Act 2005 it is inspected separately along with the teaching of denominational education where this is delivered. Often, these inspections coincide at the request of the governing body.

In short, your school would have two inspections which would probably be carried out at the same time, covering different aspects of the work of your school.

My school has specialist status. Will it be inspected in the same way?

Yes, but inspectors do have to take account of the fact that this is a special feature of your school. The lead inspector is in charge of doing this and must make sure that inspectors understand the significance of your school's specific objectives so that the team can assess how well you achieve them. Rigorous self-evaluation is a key feature of specialist school status anyway, regardless of the requirements of Ofsted. Such schools have to assess whether or not they are meeting their targets according to their development plan, so your school will be well used to such processes.

Inspectors will use the same inspection schedule as they would with any other school, and the Department for Children, Schools and Families would use the findings of the inspection, in particular the 'overall effectiveness' judgement, to inform the decision on redesignation when the time comes. In short, the main thrust of an inspection in a specialist school would be: has it met its own targets; what impact is the specialist status having on raising standards; and, what impact is the specialist status having on the community? As well as examining your school's development plan connected with its specialist status, inspectors will also want to discuss with key members of staff how far the school is going towards meeting these targets.

If you are uncertain about the way in which your school's distinctive character will impact inspection, your headteacher will be able to advise you. Your union may be able to help too.

What are the main features of school inspection?

There are several main features of school inspection, as described in the *Framework for Inspecting Schools in England from September 2005*, April 2008 edition:

- inspections that are short and focused, taking no more than two days and drawing on interaction with a school's senior leadership team as well as using the school's self-evaluation as a the starting point for the inspection;
- short notice of inspection so that inspectors get a better look at the school as it usually operates;
- inspections teams with few inspectors, many inspections being led by HMIs;
- a time period of three years between inspections, with those schools which are cause for concern being inspected more frequently;
- a strong emphasis on school improvement, drawing on a school's own self-evaluation, input from pupils, parents and others, and using this as the starting point for the inspection (this is why it is so essential for schools to stay up to date with their self-evaluation);

- common characteristics to inspection in schools;
- two categories of schools deemed to be causing concern: those requiring special measures and those requiring notice to improve.

You can find out more about these features of inspection from the Ofsted website (see below).

How frequent are school inspections?

At the time of writing schools are usually inspected on a three-year cycle.

How long will inspectors be in my school?

Inspections last no longer than two days. The number of inspectors involved in an inspection will be dependent on several factors, not least the size of your school.

Does HMI lead every inspection?

At the time of writing, no. HMI lead what is described as a 'high proportion' of secondary school inspections and a 'substantial minority' of primary school inspections. Additional inspectors make up inspection teams and you can find out more about these in Chapter 1. Additional inspectors work for inspection providers, typically private companies contracted by Ofsted to perform inspections. These inspectors are required by law to have the qualifications and experience that meet Ofsted's standards. However, HMI will be involved in the quality assurance of your school's inspection report.

What are 'reduced tariff' inspections?

These are described by Ofsted as being 'short, sharply focused' inspections. They are only performed on a percentage of schools deemed suitable as a result of analysis of a school's PANDA (or RAISEonline – see below), the latest inspection report, and 'local knowledge'. Basically, these inspections are still performed to the standard framework, but they are shorter. A report is still published in the usual way.

If you are interested in finding out more about reduced tariff inspections and how they compare with standard tariff inspections, there is a useful table in the document *Conducting the Inspection: Guidance for inspectors of schools* which is available to download from the Ofsted website (see below).

Will we be given any notice that an inspection is going to take place?

Yes, at the time of writing, schools are usually given two working days' notice. However, HMCI does have the power to authorise no-notice inspections. These would take place if there were serious concerns about the well-being or safety of pupils at the school. HMCI can also authorise inspections at his or her discretion.

What if it isn't a convenient time for an inspection? Can it be put off?

Sadly, no, not unless there is a genuine and undeniable need. Let's face it, when is inspection ever convenient? However successfully inspectors manage to minimise the negative impact on a school, they are by their very nature a 'disturbance' in that for the duration of the inspection the school is focused that way very directly (as opposed to the on-going preparedness for inspection that good schools work towards anyway). Ofsted is keen to stress that the impact on a school shouldn't be such that the normal working day is utterly disrupted, but the reality is that there *are* at least subtle changes and tweaks made to a school's operations and these all take effort and energy. It is *very* unusual for an inspection to be put off. 'Deferral' refers to inspections which are moved by more than five working days. There are very specific circumstances in which a deferral may be granted and these include, among others: the headteacher or other senior member of the leadership team being under police investigation; the very recent death of a pupil or member of staff; HMCI agreeing that inspection would cause significant disruption or distress; and at least three-quarters of pupils being planned to be absent.

You can find out more about Ofsted's deferral policy from the Ofsted website (see below).

As a head of department/curriculum leader will my subject be specifically inspected?

No, Section 5 inspections do not involve separate subject inspections. This even applies to specialist schools. Now that inspections are relatively short, there simply isn't time for inspectors to evaluate individual subjects; they have other ways of gathering information of this kind so that they can offer advice to the government on this aspect of education. They do this in the form of 'subject and aspect inspections'. These typically last a day in the primary sector and two days in the secondary sector. During these inspections, inspectors observe teaching, talk to staff and pupils and scrutinise work and documentation linked to the work of the department. These inspections are linked closely with what are thought to be issues of national importance such as the underachievement of boys.

Inspectors will be interested in the curriculum at your school, however, and will be looking at the curriculum arrangements to make sure that they not only abide by all the statutory requirements, but also that they meet the needs of your pupils and build on learning so that *progress* can be made. They will be seeking to make links between the quality of the curriculum on offer at your school and the way in which outcomes for pupils are impacted. Inspectors will discuss the curriculum with senior leaders at your school as well as with pupils. They will also be looking at the extent to which the curriculum on offer meets the needs of *all* learners, for example those with particular needs, those from specific backgrounds, and so on.

I can remember being inspected years ago and the amount of paperwork my school had to produce was ridiculous. Is it still the same now?

Things are, thankfully, very different now. The only documents your school will be asked to provide are one copy of the latest school development or improvement plan, the timetable for the school, a staff list with responsibilities indicated, times of the school day and a plan of the school; even then, if they are available on the website, inspectors should source them from there! Inspectors will also be able to access your school's SEF and RAISEonline report as well as the previous inspection report among other sources of information.

What are the grades that Ofsted use now?

At the time of writing Ofsted uses one of four grades to describe a school:

- outstanding (grade 1)
- good (grade 2)
- satisfactory (grade 3)
- inadequate (grade 4).

The 'satisfactory' grade (grade 3) is subdivided into:

- satisfactory, but improving
- satisfactory, with capacity to improve judged no better than satisfactory.

The 'inadequate' grade (grade 4) is subdivided into:

- inadequate
- notice to improve
- special measures.

Schools which are deemed to require special measures are, by definition (according to Ofsted), inadequate and with no capacity to improve.

What do the Ofsted grades actually mean?

When looking at the overall effectiveness of a school, Ofsted has defined each grade as follows:

Outstanding (1)	Exceptional: all major elements of the school's work are at least good, and significant elements are exemplary.

Good (2)	Inspectors should consider the judgement good when there is a generally strong performance across all aspects of a school's work, including the school's contribution to Every Child Matters outcomes, and the capacity to improve further is strong, as shown by its recent improvement. A school may be good in a variety of ways, and may have pockets of excellence, but no school should be judged good if its performance is merely ordinary. No school can be judged to be good unless learners are judged to make good progress.
Satisfactory (3)	The school's work is inadequate in no major area, and may be good in some respects.
Inadequate (4)	A school is likely to be inadequate if one or more of the following are judged to be inadequate: learners' achievement; learners' personal development and well-being; the overall quality of provision; leadership and management. The sixth form, boarding provision or Foundation Stage might also be inadequate but, where the numbers are small, this does not necessarily lead to the judgement that the school as a whole is inadequate. At its worst, the school provides an unacceptable standard of education and it lacks the capacity to improve.

This table and others relating to each feature of the evaluation schedule can be found in the document *Using the Evaluation Schedule: Guidance for Inspectors of Schools* (see below).

Why would a school be placed in the 'special measures' category?

Schools are placed in this category when they fail to give pupils an acceptable standard of education and there is little or no evidence that those leading the school have the capacity to facilitate the necessary improvements.

What kind of schools end up in the 'notice to improve' category?

Schools in this category are those which are deemed to be performing substantially lower than they might fairly be expected to perform. They may also be schools which are deemed to be currently failing but which have the capacity to improve.

My school is brand new. Does that mean we'll be inspected?

No, it's extremely unlikely that you would be inspected in your school's first year 'in business'. Your first inspection would typically be in your school's second year of operation.

My school has a code of conduct for the way in which teachers should behave at work. Do inspectors have to abide by something similar?

Absolutely! The inspectors that visit your school are told to uphold 'the highest professional standards in their work'. The core of this is to ensure that schools feel fairly dealt with, not to mention having the opportunity to benefit from the inspection. This is paramount as it is this opportunity which feeds school improvement. Without that, inspection is utterly invalid.

To summarise the inspectors' code of conduct, they are required to:

- be objective and impartial;
- be honest, fair and reliable in their judgements;
- work with integrity, courtesy and sensitivity;
- minimise any stress felt by those being inspected paying particular attention to well-being;
- be clear, frank and productive in their dialogues with those they are inspecting;
- be respectful of confidentiality.

The flipside of this code of conduct is that Ofsted expects those who are being inspected to be 'courteous and helpful' to inspectors.

You can find out more about the inspectors' code of conduct from the *Framework for Inspecting Schools in England from September 2005*, April 2008 edition (see below).

Are parents involved in the process at all?

Yes, Ofsted will ask schools to tell their parents that the inspection is taking place and to pass on a letter and an explanatory leaflet from Ofsted. This letter includes a confidential questionnaire which asks specifically about parents' views of the school. These are then returned (it is hoped) to the inspection team.

Some schools use their parent–teacher associations to encourage the completion of this form. As soon as notice of the inspection is given, key parents are informed who then ring around other parents and so on. The idea is to encourage a core of interested and participating parents, with a sound knowledge of the working of the school, to become involved in the inspection process. The natural by-product here is of course that these are precisely the parents who are likely to view the school and its workings in a positive light!

Another potential involvement of parents in the inspection process is that they can request to speak to inspectors while the inspection is taking place. There is no guarantee that this request will be met, but Ofsted says that inspection teams will do their best to meet them.

All the Ofsted literature for parents is available in a range of languages.

The Education and Inspections Act 2006 gives powers to Ofsted regarding complaints from parents about the school attended by their child. They can even investigate complaints made anonymously, or from people who are not registered as parents of a child at the school. However, in these circumstances, their powers of investigation are more limited. The exception to this is complaints from parents with children at independent schools. The typical kinds of complaints that may be investigated in this way include dissatisfaction with the quality of education on offer, the underachievement of pupils, a perception that the school is wasting money, poor leadership and management, and too little regard to pupils' well-being and safety. Ofsted, however, does not mediate in disputes between schools and parents, nor does it get involved in investigating incidents that may have taken place and judging how well a school dealt with them.

Why do we need published inspection reports? Is this really necessary? Surely it's better for the school to be informed of the outcome of an inspection privately?

Inspection reports are published to give parents, schools and the wider community information about the quality of education on offer at a particular school. These reports also give information on whether inspectors believe that pupils are achieving as much as they can at the school. Whatever your thoughts on the validity of the inspectors' views, this is certainly, in theory, information that is of interest to the general public.

When will our report be available?

Your school will receive its report in writing within ten working days after the end of the inspection. Once your school receives the report, it has ten working days to give parents a summary of the report's findings. Interestingly, your school has to provide a summary of the report to anyone who requests it free of charge. It also has to provide a copy of the full report to anyone who requests it but it may charge copying costs for this. The report would typically go up on the Ofsted website within 15 working days from the end of the inspection. School holidays, of course, can disrupt all this. In this case, schools have longer to make their reports available.

What is RAISEonline?

This is Reporting and Analysis for Improvement through School self-Evaluation. It replaces the old PANDA (Ofsted Performance and Assessment) and the PAT (Pupil and Achievement Tracker). In essence, RAISEonline is a tool to make it easier for schools to keep track of the latest data and to explore it in depth, right down to the level of individual pupils. In this respect it is a one-stop shop for school data and analysis and really helps schools to enter the self-evaluation process in greater depth and detail. It can also support target-setting and the investigation and/or exploration of hypotheses about pupil performance, among other things.

Your headteacher will be able to tell you more about the way in which RAISEonline is used in your school. It isn't essential or mandatory for schools to use it, although many do. There are other methods of data analysis which can help with self-evaluation. You can also find out more about RAISEonline from the Ofsted website (see below) and also from the RAISEonline website (see below).

What is the self-evaluation form?

The self-evaluation form, or SEF, is a framework in which schools can explore 'strengths and weaknesses'. It has close links with RAISEonline and other methods of data analysis because Ofsted requires schools to provide evidence for its self-evaluations and these are just the kind of tools which can help schools in this.

Ofsted is keen to stress that it believes that schools are best placed to identify their own strengths and development needs. This is what lies at the heart of school self-evaluation. Part of this, though, is that schools identify for themselves what they might do about improving what needs improving and developing what needs developing.

The main vehicle that schools have for facilitating this self-evaluation is the SEF, and it is the main document that inspectors use when planning their inspections because it is very important in the evaluation of the quality of a school's leadership and management, as well as the school's ability to improve. This is the document that inspectors will be poring over before they arrive at your school on the first day of inspection.

Schools can edit the SEF as many times as they like although it will be 'locked' soon after notice of inspection is given so that inspectors have a chance to examine it before the inspection begins. For this reason it is essential for schools to take an on-going 'work in progress' attitude towards self-evaluation because it simply cannot be done at the last minute. All maintained and some non-maintained schools can use the SEF. If you want to find out more about your school's SEF, speak to your headteacher, who will be able to talk you through it.

Interestingly, since 2005 and the introduction of a much stronger focus on self-evaluation, Ofsted has seen a growth in confidence in the ways in which schools are able to handle performance data in order both to establish their priorities for development and to evaluate their own progress. It seems that placing self-evaluation at the heart of inspection has been very beneficial.

You can also find out more about the SEF from the Ofsted website (see below).

Is it true that inspection is more about leadership and management than it is about the rest of what goes on in schools?

While inspection does look closely at leadership and management, that is by no means the full extent of what goes on. Inspectors will want to make sure that your senior leadership team is accurate and effective in its self-evaluation and monitoring and that the targets the school sets for itself do actually lead to improvements, but that is just part of the overall inspection. They will also want to see that professional development targets are appropriate to the needs of the school and individuals. It is *impact* on *progress* that inspectors are particularly interested in. All members of staff are part of the school team and are, in effect, all being inspected.

What is the common inspection schedule for schools and other post-16 provision?

The common inspection schedule comprises the questions that inspectors have to ask in every institution and setting providing education and/or training. Inspections of educational settings (apart from those which only offer adult education) feed into joint area reviews which are carried out in local authorities every three years. The purpose of these joint area reviews is to establish the extent to which each area is meeting the five outcomes of the Every Child Matters agenda for children and young people (see below). These are:

- being healthy
- staying safe
- enjoying and achieving
- making a positive contribution
- achieving economic well-being.

When inspectors visit your school to judge leadership and management and the overall effectiveness of the school, they will be looking really closely at the extent to which your school contributes to helping children and young people achieve all five outcomes. Do not underestimate the importance of the Every Child Matters agenda to Ofsted inspection. This is precisely the sort of activity which is implicit in the work of schools but which has to be spelled out to inspectors. Don't ever assume that they will notice something you want them to notice: tell them about it. Tell them, and show them the evidence for, what a great contribution your school makes every day to helping children achieve those outcomes.

So what, exactly, do inspectors evaluate?

What follows is the common inspection schedule for schools and other post-16 provision. Notice how it clearly identifies how the five outcomes of the Every Child Matters agenda are covered by the schedule. You can find what follows in the *Framework for Inspecting Schools in England from September 2005*, April 2008 edition (see below):

Overall effectiveness

How effective and efficient are the provision and related services in meeting the full range of learners' needs and why?[1]

What steps need to be taken to improve the provision further?

Inspectors should evaluate:

- the overall effectiveness of the provision, including any specialist provision and extended services, and its main strengths and weaknesses;
- the capacity to make further improvements;
- the effectiveness of any steps taken to promote improvement since the last inspection;

and, where appropriate:

- the effectiveness of links with other organisations to promote the well-being of learners;
- the effectiveness of the Foundation Stage;
- the effectiveness of the sixth form.

Achievement and standards

How well do learners achieve?

Inspectors should evaluate (the numbers in parentheses refer to the Every Child Matters outcomes in each part of the schedule):

- learners' success in achieving challenging targets, including qualifications and learning goals, with trends over time and any significant variations between groups of learners (3);
- the standards of learners' work (3);
- learners' progress relative to their prior attainment and potential, with any significant variations between groups of learners (3);
- the extent to which learners enjoy their work (3);

BOX CONTINUES OVERLEAF

1 More detailed listings of what to evaluate are given in *Using the Evaluation Schedule.*

and, where appropriate: [2]

- the acquisition of workplace skills (4,5);
- the development of skills which contribute to the social and economic well-being of the learner (2,4,5);
- the emotional development of learners (1);
- the behaviour of learners (1,2);
- the attendance of learners (2,3);
- the extent to which learners adopt safe practices and a healthy lifestyle (1,2,5);
- learners' spiritual, moral, social and cultural development (3,4);
- whether learners make a positive contribution to the community (4).

The quality of provision

How effective are teaching, training and learning?

Inspectors should evaluate:

- how well teaching and/or training and resources promote learning, address the full range of learners' needs and meet course or programme requirements (3,4);
- the suitability and rigour of assessment in planning and monitoring learners' progress (3);
- the identification of, and provision for, additional learning needs (3);

and, where appropriate:

- the involvement of parents and carers in their children's learning and development (3).

How well do programmes and activities meet the needs and interests of learners?

Inspectors should evaluate:

- the extent to which programmes or activities match learners' needs, aspirations and potential, building on prior attainment and experience (3,5);

2 These outcomes for learners are generally reported in the personal development and well-being section of Section 5 school reports.

- how far programmes or the curriculum meet external requirements and are responsive to local circumstances (4,5);
- the extent to which enrichment activities and/or extended services contribute to learners' enjoyment and achievement (3,4,5);
- the extent to which the provision contributes to the learners' personal development and well-being, for example their capacity to stay safe and healthy, and their spiritual, moral, social and cultural development (1, 2).

How well are learners guided and supported?
Inspectors should evaluate:

- the care, advice, guidance and other support provided to safeguard welfare, promote personal development and achieve high standards (1,2,3);
- the quality and accessibility of information, advice and guidance to learners in relation to courses and programmes, and where applicable, career progression (3,5).

Leadership and management
How effective are leadership and management in raising achievement and supporting all learners?
Inspectors should evaluate:

- how effectively self-evaluation is used to secure improvement;
- how well challenging targets are being used to raise standards for all learners;
- how effectively leaders and managers at all levels clearly direct improvement and promote the well-being of learners through high quality care, education and training;
- how well equality of opportunity is promoted and discrimination tackled so that all learners achieve their potential;
- the adequacy and suitability of staff, including the effectiveness of processes for recruitment and selection of staff to ensure that learners are well taught and protected;
- the adequacy and suitability of specialist equipment, learning resources and accommodation;

BOX CONTINUES OVERLEAF

- how effectively and efficiently resources are deployed to achieve value for money.

and, where appropriate:

- how effective are the links made with other providers, services, employers and other organisations to promote the integration of care, education and any extended services to enhance learning and to promote well-being;
- the effectiveness with which governors and other supervisory boards discharge their responsibilities.

A really positive way of using this schedule as a teacher is to go through and aim to identify in your work what you do to contribute to each aspect of it. This wouldn't actually happen, but if you had an inspector in front of you now, could you go through this schedule and describe what you do in your classroom and beyond that might lead an inspector to conclude that your part in the schedule is either good or outstanding? Don't get hung up on this kind of exercise; it's just a tool to encourage you to link your work directly with the features of school life that inspectors are particularly interested in.

So what is the importance of the Every Child Matters agenda?

It's very important. Inspectors are told to give 'prominence' to the five outcomes of the Every Child Matters agenda and will be looking for evidence so that they can report on them. Overall, the inspectors will be looking to ensure that your school is effective in its contribution towards these five outcomes. Often they do this through taking 'case studies' of vulnerable children, as identified by your school. Sometimes inspectors will want to talk to these children but are asked to do so as part of a larger group so that the individuals concerned don't feel 'singled out'.

The overall report will clearly evaluate the five outcomes in the sections on achievement and standards and on personal development and well-being.

When it comes to the inspection of a school, what does Ofsted have to report on?

Ofsted has certain statutory responsibilities concerning its inspection of schools which include reporting on:

- the quality of the education provided in the school;
- how far the education provided in the school meets the needs of the range of children and young people at the school;
- the educational standards achieved in the school;
- the quality of the leadership and management of the school, including whether the financial resources made available to the school are managed effectively;
- the spiritual, moral, social and cultural development of pupils at the school;
- the contribution made by the school to the well-being of the pupils.

That, in short, is what Ofsted inspection in schools is all about! It is worth keeping in mind that as far as achievement is concerned, inspectors are interested in *progress* made more than anything. Always keep that in mind.

What are the basic issues that Ofsted is looking at during an inspection?

Ofsted says that there are some very basic questions which need to be asked when judging any school. These questions are:

- What is the overall effectiveness of the school?
- What is its capacity to improve?
- What is the quality of learning in the school? Are all the children and young people making the progress and attaining the standards they should?
- Is the well-being of children and young people promoted appropriately and are their views being valued?

- Are the leadership and management effective in ensuring that:
  - the teaching is consistently effective and has a positive impact on quality?
  - equality, diversity and community cohesion are taken into account?
  - the views of parents and children and young people are listened to and acted upon?
  - the curriculum meets the needs of all learners?
  - resources are adequate and used well?
  - all learners are supported effectively?
- What are the key actions that will help the school to achieve further improvement?

What do inspectors use their time in schools for if they have gathered evidence in advance?

Inspectors have to use their time in school to gather first-hand evidence of how your school operates and the quality of education it offers its pupils to feed into the conclusions they make about how effective your school is. The evidence that inspectors gather will be recorded on evidence forms which are used to help reach corporate judgements. These judgements must be made on each section of the inspection schedule for schools and are recorded by the lead inspector in the Inspection Judgements Form. Judgements have to be supported by convincing evidence.

When your school is inspected you should expect to see inspectors talking to staff and pupils, observing lessons, exploring school processes, looking at policies, analysing samples of pupils' work, observing meetings and other management processes, seeing examples of school life such as school council meetings, analysing pupil records, and tracking specific case studies such as children looked after or those with learning difficulties.

I know that teachers should be accountable for their work, but I don't actually know what that means in the context of my work. How can I get beneath the confusion to a greater understanding?

The question of to whom and to what teachers are accountable cannot easily be answered. It would seem that teachers must follow the steps of a complex dance, the tune to which may be provided by their school leaders, governor, local authorities, parents, pupils, Ofsted, the General Teaching Councils, the Department for Children, Schools and Families and so on, and so on. In an ideal world this would be a tune of beautiful harmony but is this the experience of most teachers? Not really. In fact, many might say that what they hear is a cacophony! There is also quite a large degree of duplication in accountability when school improvement partners, league tables and the new relationship with schools are taken into consideration too.

Ofsted inspections focus the minds of teachers and parents on national and local accountability, and not least on the fact that schools are a public service using tremendous amounts of public money. This focus is heightened by the publication of a written report on each school.

The fact that accountability is a necessary part of professional life is not in question, but knowing who you, as a teacher, are accountable to, is. For the purposes of inspection do not focus on the wider (public) picture of accountability. Just stay focused on your work in your school with your pupils. Know the boundaries within which you are expected to operate and work to the best of your ability. That is all that can be expected of you.

There is more on the notion of accountability in Chapter 5, which you may find useful.

I've heard some people say some pretty damning things about inspection which I'm sure cannot be what the system is all about. What is inspection not about?

It's absolutely right to give some thought to what inspection is *not*. Quite naturally there is some suspicion about the system because of its very nature; having an outside agency assess your work is challenging in any profession, but we do need to encourage and nurture perspective. It has been said many times before but it's worth stating it again, inspection is a 'snapshot' of your work as a teacher at that time. It does not define or delineate your future career, and does not place restrictions on the scope of your future development as a teacher. Indeed even as the inspection report is being published it will be out of date, particularly if you work in a dynamic institution which responds to the needs of its members.

Inspection is not a fault-finding exercise and the judgements made should certainly not be carried for an eternity. For inspection to be most useful to schools and their pupils, teachers must be able to take from them what will promote development and shake off anything else!

What is the pre-inspection briefing (PIB)? Is that something I have to be involved in?

The pre-inspection briefing is an evaluative document that is required as part of the evidence base for inspections. It gives the inspection team a preliminary view of the school based on the evidence available so far, and it tells the school what the inspectors will be following up in detail when they visit. It is an incredibly important document in that it provides a starting point for discussions between the school and the inspection team on the most important issues.

As a class teacher, you won't be involved in the PIB at all unless your school's senior leadership team needs you to help them provide additional evidence as a result of finding out what the focus of the inspection is. If you have a role in the school which is pertinent to the main focus of the inspection, you may be asked to take part in discussions with inspectors.

Basically, the PIB helps the inspection to get off to a clear and focused start without wasting any time in the few days that inspectors are in school. It also helps to make sure that the inspection is focused within the framework of the Every Child Matters agenda. The PIB doesn't make pre-emptive judgements for the inspection. Rather, it helps inspectors to focus their thoughts towards hypotheses and issues to be pursued during the inspection. It is the PIB combined with the SEF which forms the basis of the pre-inspection briefing. Inspectors are told to be flexible though, and not to be rigid in their planned activities while in a school. They must be able to reshape what they do during the course of their visit if that is what is needed. Your school should receive the PIB for your inspection by 16.00 on the day before the inspection.

How will inspectors remember everything they do and see while they are in my school?

A lot of the pre-inspection data (such as the self-evaluation form) is written down and inspectors must also record all the meetings they have with staff members on evidence forms (even down to the final meetings they have and the final feedback to the school). There shouldn't be any room for error, but if mistakes are made, you do have a right to ask for them to be corrected.

What goes into the written inspection report?

According to the *Framework for Inspecting Schools in England from September 2005*, April 2008 edition (see below), every Ofsted inspection report must include:

- a commentary on the school's effectiveness, its strengths and weaknesses, what it must do to improve, and the parents' and pupils' views of the school;
- all of the evaluation requirements specified in the common inspection schedule for schools and other post-16 provision.

The report is in a set format although the content should be utterly unique and specific to your school. It should also, it goes without saying, be factually accurate. To help ensure that this is so, schools get the chance to check the pre-publication draft of the inspection report (although only one working day is allocated to this task unless your school is in a category of concern). Only factual errors can be changed at this point. Judgements are set in stone! Interestingly the main intended audience for the report is parents of children at your school.

I've heard that inspectors also write to pupils at the schools they inspect. Is this true?

Yes it is. Inspectors write a brief letter to pupils summarising the main findings of the inspection and this usually becomes an annex to the final report. They will/should write it in language suitable for the ages of pupils at your school so that it is accessible for the *majority*. HMCI does expect that schools will do all in their power to inform pupils of the outcome of the inspection. Obviously this has to be done in an appropriate way in order for it to have meaning for young people.

I've heard that inspectors are supposed to make a judgement on whether a school offers value for money. What does that mean and how on earth can they make those kinds of judgements?

When inspectors are looking at the value for money provided by your school they will be weighing up the income the school receives for each learner against the outcomes that are achieved at the school and the overall quality of what is provided by your school. It isn't a foregone conclusion, but the chances are that a school which is deemed to be inadequate (grade 4) will also be deemed to be providing unsatisfactory value for money. Those schools which are graded 1–3 are likely to be deemed to be offering satisfactory value for money.

Does Ofsted inspect any schools outside England?

Very few. In fact the only schools it inspects outside England are service children's schools for the Ministry of Defence.

How can I, as a teacher, know that any inspection of my school is going to be of a high quality? As teachers we have to provide quality, but what about inspectors?

This is a very important question and one that schools need to have answered satisfactorily in order to feel a valid part of the process of inspection. As you head into an inspection, know that the quality of inspections and reports is assessed by HMI. HMI also assesses the effectiveness of additional inspectors and the quality assurance arrangements of the regional contractors that are used to undertake inspections (see Chapter 1). These arrangements may see inspectors being monitored and if a report is deemed to be misleading or flawed the school concerned may be offered another inspection. This is one reason why quality assurance is so incredibly important!

After your inspection, your school will also be invited to take part in a post-inspection survey. This will request the views of headteachers, staff and governors among others on the recent inspection and the aim is for these to feed into the positive development of inspections. If you feel strongly about contributing to the post-inspection survey, speak to your headteacher.

You can find out more about the post-inspection survey from the *Framework for Inspecting Schools in England from September 2005*, April 2008 edition (see below).

Is there a complaints procedure concerning school inspection?

Yes there is. It is worth pointing out here that according to Ofsted, the vast majority of inspections go off without a hitch and are free of complaint. That said, there is a procedure which can be followed in the event of a school needing to complain about any aspect of their inspection. Information on this procedure can be downloaded from the Ofsted website (see below) and there is more on making complaints in Chapter 8. Concerns about the way in which an inspection is being carried out are usually dealt with quickly and easily during the course of the inspection. Schools are encouraged to raise their concerns with the lead inspector and Ofsted will step in and advise on this process should the need arise.

What if my school is deemed to be inadequate after the inspection? Will I still have a job?

The outcome of an inspection should not affect your employment rights. If you have development needs which your headteacher or line manager is more aware of as a result of the inspection you should be offered suitable support and training. If there are serious competency questions, your school will have a procedure for dealing with these. If you are in any doubt at all about any of these issues, your union will be able to support you.

Find out more ...

- The Ofsted website can be accessed via: www.ofsted.gov.uk
- RAISEonline can be accessed here: www.raiseonline.org
- The *Framework for Inspecting Schools in England from September 2005*, April 2008 edition, can be downloaded free of charge from the Ofsted website: www.ofsted.gov.uk
- The *Every Child Matters Agenda* can be viewed online at: www.every-childmatters.gov.uk
- *Using the Evaluation Schedule: Guidance for Inspectors of Schools* is available to download from the Ofsted website: www.ofsted.gov.uk
- *Conducting the Inspection: Guidance for Inspectors of Schools* is available to download from the Ofsted website: www.ofsted.gov.uk

CHAPTER 3

Being inspection-aware

> Nothing would be done at all if a man waited until he could do it so well that no one could find fault with it.
>
> Cardinal Newman

Introduction

At any one time there will be a significant number of teachers who have never experienced an Ofsted inspection. Whether this is because they have only recently qualified, or have missed it by chance through changing jobs, there's no doubt that this can create anxiety, not to mention an air of mystery around the whole process. Being inspection-aware, even in the most general of terms, can help to demystify what Ofsted is all about and help to ensure that when the event does happen, it is simply experienced as a potentially useful feature of life in a school.

We may be forgiven for expecting that the dawn of reduced-notice inspections should have heralded a dramatically reduced stress response in schools! No longer are we taking months to prepare for the inspectors' visit. Now, it's all about short notice and relatively short inspections. Has this helped? Yes, of course, but there is still a need to be 'inspection-aware' so that you are ready for this important aspect of teaching in a school and not overwhelmed by the thought of it. On-going preparedness is what it's all about now.

This chapter explores ideas around:

- the advantages of inspection;
- the ever-ready approach to inspection;
- preparation for Ofsted;
- matching the common inspection schedule to your work;
- strengths and weaknesses;
- spiritual, moral, social and cultural development of pupils;
- utilising professional dialogues and professional learning teams;
- reading Ofsted reports;
- the teachers' role in inspection;
- performance management records;
- community cohesion.

What are the advantages of having a system of inspection?

Having had many conversations with heads, teachers, inspectors, parents, governors, pupils and so on it does seem to me that there are several universally held ideas about the advantages that having a system of school inspection can hold for schools and their teachers. These include:

- encouragement to focus on accountability issues;
- the recognition of knowledge and skills;
- their confidence-building features – they can be a boost for all staff, bringing them together in a common purpose;
- encouragement of further development of skills, in particular improved management systems – in short, they can be a catalyst for change;
- they focus the mind on what is working and what is not, encouraging self-review and peer review through the examination of content and delivery of lessons;
- they can inspire organisation of the physical environment;
- the findings of an inspection can affirm the direction that a school is taking or illuminate future directions;
- evidence of good work and achievements can be made public;
- relationships between colleagues can flourish through the grace and camaraderie needed when a team is under scrutiny;

- they can question our sense of security in what we do, which can lead to positive and creative responses;
- they can be empowering if a commitment to change is needed and then harnessed;
- they can highlight change over time;
- use of an inspection system means that other methods of success measurement, such as educational output, are not solely relied upon.

I feel as though I have to be 'battle-ready' all the time when it comes to Ofsted. I know that we haven't been inspected as a school for a while so it's inevitably going to be in the next academic year. What's the best way of retaining a helpful perspective on this?

Thinking of it as being 'battle-ready' isn't a useful analogy. Yes, you do have to factor in a visit from Ofsted in the not too distant future, but how about viewing it as a chance to talk about and demonstrate all the great teaching that goes on in your classroom all the time, and not just during an inspection? All you need to do is what you routinely do to achieve high standards of teaching and learning and retain a sound balance between complacency and panic! It's human nature that we're unlikely to be able to identify for ourselves if we are venturing too far into the realms of complacency, in which case inspection serves an excellent purpose in gently pointing out what requires our attention, but we will certainly know if we are starting to panic about things. If you find yourself tipping too far in this direction these ideas will help:

- Talk to colleagues to help retain a balanced perspective. It's likely that you share the same concerns and knowing that you aren't alone is strengthening.
- Aim to deal with specific issues and concerns as they arise rather than panicking to cope with them once the inspection begins. For example, if there is a child or group of children that concerns you with regard to inspection and what inspectors may make of your handling of them, seek professional development advice sooner rather than later. Talk to your line manager about solution-focused training. The more equipped

you are to combat your classroom concerns, the more free and relaxed you can feel about having inspectors in to see how you operate.

- Forget any ideas about perfection. There's no such thing! Every school is a work in progress, and so is every classroom. Show that you know where you've come from, where you're going and why and you can't really go wrong. You've heard of the notion of the 'good enough' parent? Well the same concept applies to just about every aspect of life!

Do I have to do any specific preparation for inspection?

No! There is no requirement whatsoever for schools to do any specific preparation for Ofsted inspection. The Self-Evaluation Form is available for schools to complete on an on-going basis and inspectors will use this to help inform their visit to a school but they do *not* require any other additional paperwork.

However, the reality is that in the course of showing an inspection team just what a school is all about, what it achieves and how well it supports its pupils, it will want to provide documentary evidence. This is entirely at the school's discretion.

Something else you might like to consider is taking a close look at the common inspection schedule which is on pp. 37–40 and matching your work as closely as you can to what it is that the inspectors will be looking at when they visit your school. This is a great way of becoming familiar with what inspectors will be doing in your school and getting into the habit of being inspection-aware.

If I look at the Ofsted common inspection schedule and aim to match it where possible to my own work at school, how will I know what I'm doing is any good?

The key here is not to get paralysed by it all, but to use a little knowledge of the process of inspection to your advantage. A really useful document to use in this exercise is called *Using the Evaluation Schedule: Guidance for Inspectors of Schools*. This is available to download from the Ofsted website (see below). This handy little document offers inspectors guidance on how to make the evaluations they have to make. In other words, it details exactly what outstanding, good, satisfactory and inadequate look like in every aspect of the evaluation schedule. It cannot be stressed enough how useful this document can be in totally demystifying any aspect of the inspection! Download it now!

It is important to have the attitude that inspections are performed *with* a school and not *to* a school. It's a subtle shift in perception but one which will help you experience it in a far more positive and constructive way.

I'm OK with the idea of strengths being identified but 'weakness' is such a difficult word! How can I feel better about the potential for being told about my weaknesses?

There would be very little point in inspecting a school specifically to uncover weaknesses, regardless of any strengths that may exist. That said, there would also be no point in going through an inspection only to be told that you are doing well, with no regard to what aspects might be improved. In the process of establishing a judgement on the quality of education that is delivered at your school, inspectors will identify key strengths and development needs (or weaknesses). Perhaps it is a reflection of human nature that we tend to cling onto the weaknesses as the defining feature of our work, while glossing over all our positive achievements. Whatever the nature of the development needs that are highlighted as a result of the inspection at your school, always keep in mind that those needs cannot be met by one person alone and that you, as an individual, are part of a team!

Is Ofsted still interested in the spiritual, moral, social and cultural development of pupils? If so, how can I prepare for that?

Yes, the spiritual, moral, social and cultural development of pupils at your school will be a feature of any inspections you experience. This is actually an important aspect of inspection about which much has been written. There are inherent difficulties for anyone having to make judgements on these aspects of pupils' development, not least because such an assessment must necessarily be limited by the spiritual, moral, social and cultural (SMSC) development of the assessors (i.e. inspectors) and professional perspectives will naturally differ. There remains little consensus of opinion on what constitutes, for example, 'spiritual development'.

SMSC development must (and usually does) underpin all education to varying degrees. It must also be capable of engaging pupils on many levels, particularly cognitively, experientially and emotionally. Yet it can be difficult, when seeking to review exactly how pupils can develop in this way, to ascertain what is meant by spiritual, social, moral and cultural (especially 'spiritual') and whether or not they can in fact be measured. Personal growth is an enormously complex notion that does not sit happily in any one area of the curriculum. Rather, every aspect of a school's curriculum can take responsibility for SMSC development.

This book cannot afford the space to do justice to this vitally important aspect of school life. SMSC development carries high educational ideals and it is an area of school life that many teachers pride themselves on, despite the fact that these aspects of education are rarely planned as scrupulously as other subjects are. The other side of this coin, sadly, can be bafflement at what a teacher and the school as a whole are supposed to do to ensure that pupils receive this vital development.

SMSC development cannot happen if left to chance, and inspectors will be looking out for this. Pupils cannot be relied upon to 'catch' this education merely through example and observation. Pupils who are fearful of sanctions as a result of antisocial behaviour show no proof of social (or any other) development.

Some proponents of SMSC development in schools believe that through every interaction with staff members, in every lesson and every assembly, pupils need to be taught (and shown how to appreciate) the qualities that will facilitate this development. This means that your provision of spiritual, moral, social and cultural development needs to be specific and identifiable (and made explicit in any documentation for which you have responsibility).

The Ofsted document, *Using the Evaluation Schedule: Guidance for Inspectors of Schools*, outlines what inspectors would consider to be outstanding, good, satisfactory and inadequate in relation to evaluating personal development and well-being (see the table overleaf). It's worth becoming familiar with this as it is so closely connected with the five outcomes of the Every Child Matters agenda too (see below). Take a look at the table below and think about how you can have an impact on this particular judgement. This exercise will also help you to see just what you are already achieving! And remember, make explicit what is implicit in the way in which your run your classroom and teach your pupils. As well as emotional intelligence, what's the moral intelligence in your classroom?

In order to make these judgements, inspectors will need to talk to pupils, parents, governors and staff members as well as making their own observations of lessons, assemblies, behaviour and so on. When talking to pupils, they will want to know whether they feel safe or whether they are generally troubled by life at school.

Evaluating personal development and well-being

Outstanding (1)	Learners' personal development and well-being are at least good in all major respects and are exemplary in significant elements.
Good (2)	Learners' overall spiritual, moral, social and cultural development is good, and no element of it is unsatisfactory. Young children are learning to understand their feelings. All learners enjoy school a good deal, as demonstrated by their considerate behaviour, positive attitudes and regular attendance. They feel safe, are safety conscious without being fearful, and they adopt healthy lifestyles. They develop a commitment to racial equality. They make good overall progress in developing the personal qualities that will enable them to contribute effectively to the community and eventually to their working life.
Satisfactory (3)	Learners' personal development and their well-being are inadequate in no major respect, and may be good in some respects.

BOX CONTINUES OVERLEAF

Inadequate (4)	Learners' overall spiritual, moral, social and cultural development is unsatisfactory. Learners in general, or significant groups of them, are disaffected and do not enjoy their education, as shown by their unsatisfactory attitudes, behaviour and attendance, so that they do not learn effectively. Too many require internal and external exclusion. Some groups of learners are isolated or integrate poorly with other learners. Exposure to bullying, racial discrimination or other factors means that learners feel unsafe. When threatened, they do not have confidence that they can get sufficient support. Healthy lifestyles are not adequately appreciated or pursued. Learners do not engage readily with the community. Learners are not developing the social and learning skills that will equip them for work.

I feel quite intimidated by the 'spiritual' element of the SMSC development of children and young people. How can I demystify this? I'm sure I'm not as inadequate in this area as I sometimes think I am!

You are almost certainly not inadequate in this area. It is perhaps the most problematic to ensure the spiritual development of pupils while they are in your care, probably because the concept of 'spirit' is so difficult to define and so connected by its association with religion. At its most simple (yet what follows is by no means definitive), spirituality is about relationship with oneself, with others, with a higher self and/or with (a) God, and with nature. The following ideas may help, as may the opinions of a trusted colleague on the nature of spirituality in your classroom:

- Do you encourage a sense of awe and wonder in pupils regarding their existence and what surrounds them, irrespective of religious belief?

- Do you have a sense of awe and wonder at what you are teaching?
- Are your pupils offered stimulating work that can ignite their imaginations? Is there work that embraces the cognitive, experiential and emotional?
- Are all aspects of human existence celebrated as welcome and valid experiences? Is it safe for pupils to express emotions such as joy, hope, grief, anger and love? Are there any ways you can nurture this through your work in the classroom, perhaps through circle time (which, when used correctly, has a valid place in classrooms for learners of all ages)?
- Can the drama of life be discussed in your classroom? What is the 'story' behind the concepts you are teaching?
- Can you use drama and/or role-playing to enable pupils to 'be' someone or something different, or to compare their existence with another's?
- Are pupils free to 'go with the flow'? Can they develop appropriate detachment?
- Do you know what your pupils' goals and aspirations are? Do *they* know? Do they have the opportunities to discover what those may be?
- Do your pupils 'discover' some of the knowledge they gain?
- Is there any piece of art, music or literature that can add depth to your work in the classroom, regardless of the subject you teach?
- Can the natural environment be brought into your teaching? Is a deep respect for nature and the natural world something that underpins your teaching?
- Can your pupils feel the 'passion' of what you are teaching them? Are you able to 'raise their spirits'? Do you feel 'spiritually and creatively alive'?
- Are pupils allowed a quiet time or period of silence when in your classroom, in order to focus, uninterrupted, on the work they are doing and 'connect' to it?
- Do you have a clear understanding of what characteristics would signify 'spiritual development' in your pupils?
- If asked, would you be able to give examples of 'spiritual development' that has taken place in your classroom?

- Do you know what aspects of the curriculum that you teach lend themselves most effectively to spiritual development?
- There are some key concepts such as awe, wonder, vivacity, courage, hope, enthusiasm, wholeness, loyalty, uniqueness, inspiration, peace, joy, creativity, empathy, humour, imagination, curiosity, caring, openness, pride, privacy, individuality and spontaneity which can help to support spiritual development in children and young people. In what ways do they feature in your classroom?

Spirituality in schools should not, indeed cannot, simply be provided through religious education. There is not a single curriculum area that can escape the potential role in nurturing spirituality in pupils beyond the textbooks. Admittedly, some subject areas will lend themselves more easily to this, particularly the humanities, social sciences and arts subjects (although science and maths hold a whole lot of awe and wonder!) but if it was not for a quest-like spirit in the founders of other areas of study, they simply would not exist as we know them today.

Do not be put off by feelings that your pupils may be too disenfranchised to benefit from any attention to spirit. Even small steps in this direction can have tremendously positive outcomes, and to be starved of spiritual nourishment at school is crippling indeed.

The concept of spirit seems to have captured our imaginations right now. Mind, body and spirit books are ever-popular, as are the associated DVDs, workshops and seminars. Take, for example, the BBC Two programme *The Monastery* which was broadcast in the UK in 2005–6. The series followed five men who were chosen from 250 applicants to live alongside the Benedictine monks at Worth Abbey in West Sussex. As a result of the programme, many thousands contacted the Abbey for guidance on how to enhance the spirituality they experienced in their daily lives, and the Open Cloister programme run by Worth Abbey developed as a result.

Spiritual awareness is becoming more accessible to a greater number of people and is being presented to children in ever more attractive ways. Your work in the classroom can build on the spiritual development that pupils will be gaining (to a greater or lesser degree) outside school. Yet it is less about adding to the existing content of your lessons and schemes of work, and more about ensuring that the content as it stands carries *meaning*.

The spiritual, moral, social and cultural development that takes place in schools is not always reported in inspection reports as thoroughly as it might be, and is perhaps the hardest area for Ofsted to crack in terms of having a positive impact (although links to the outcomes of the Every Child Matters agenda certainly help). If this is a strength of yours, or a strength that you are working towards as a classroom teacher or a school as a whole, you would be justified in making a song and dance about it! It should be remembered though that the *process* of spiritual, moral, social and cultural education is at least, if not more, significant than the *outcome*.

I feel that we should be benefiting more in my school from each other. There is a lot of expertise on the staff but we rarely share it. Surely being inspection-aware is linked into this? If we get in the habit of professional dialogues with each other, we'll enhance our on-going readiness for inspection, won't we?

Professional dialogues between staff members are an essential part of any school's professional development and consequently of a school's readiness for inspection. They have been shown to be one of the most effective professional development tools within the school environment and are incredibly cost-effective too! The success of professional dialogues seems to lie in the mutual vulnerability of those involved. When that is present, true professional learning can be facilitated.

If your school is not in the habit of encouraging professional dialogues between staff, perhaps raise the possibility at a staff meeting. Aim to include governors in this process too. There don't need to be set formulas for holding these dialogues, but it can help to schedule them and at the very least pre-arrange a topic or issue for discussion. Although referred to as dialogues, more than two people can successfully be involved, as long as each takes to the discussion a desire to give and take in the purpose of learning: hence the need for mutual vulnerability.

You may also want to consider setting up professional learning teams in your school as well. These seem to be a really effective way of improving the quality of teaching and learning that a school offers and are relatively easy to get up and running. The main thrust of a professional learning team is that members collectively work towards improving professional learning. Some schools even go as far as organising Ofsted learning teams, whose focus it is to disseminate learning which will support teachers and other staff members in the event of an inspection. This kind of approach helps schools be inspection-ready, ensuring that inspectors aren't an unwelcome surprise, but expected guests.

There is no perfect way to set up professional learning teams in your school; an element of trial and error will help you to settle on a formula that works best for you in the context in which you work. A good structure to follow is to nominate a leader of learning for each team who then has the task of directing the work of the team in a strategic way. This helps to ensure focus and progress; two vital targets of a professional learning team. As a team, you would set out desired roadmaps to achieving the goals you set for yourselves and the school. The kinds of questions you would be asking as a team, therefore, are the what, when, how, from where and why questions.

If your school is new to using professional learning teams, do be aware that they can be somewhat chaotic to set up. These ideas may help to reduce the potential for chaos:

- The size of the team is important; a team of about four or five members works well. Aim for the make-up of the team to be as inter-disciplinary as possible.
- Meet regularly! It sounds obvious, but unless you meet on a regular basis to discuss progress and future direction, you're unlikely to be of much practical use. Keep these meetings orientated to *action* too.
- Make sure that each member of the team knows exactly what is expected of them. These teams work best if expectations are both agreed and shared, with improvements in teaching and learning being the main aim.
- Be sure to identify training needs within the professional learning team, particularly in respect of an imminent inspection.

- Reflection is an important feature of professional learning teams. You can find out more about how this can be achieved in relation to an Ofsted inspection in Chapter 9. Aim to build in mutual support too.
- This isn't a clique; make sure that the professional learning team is transparent to others and that the learning acquired is accessible to all.

The National College for School Leadership website carries information on using professional learning teams in schools. See below to find out more.

I have never been through an inspection before and I know very little about what goes on. I'd like to read some published Ofsted reports. Where can I access these?

Reading recent Ofsted reports is a great way of becoming familiar with what the system of inspection is all about. It doesn't matter if you don't know the actual schools; just getting a feel for what is covered and what isn't, the language used in the reports, their length and overall tone gives you useful background information.

You can access Ofsted reports on the Ofsted website (see below). If you go to the homepage and click on 'Inspection reports' you will find a search facility.

I feel as though I will have to show inspectors everything I do and demonstrate the knowledge that my pupils have. It's quite a paralysing thought! What is my role when inspectors arrive?

Don't invent work for yourself. Inspection is simply about how your school operates on a normal day-to-day basis, not how many tricks it can pull out of the bag for the benefit of inspectors! Yes, it is helpful if you are ready, willing and able to talk to inspectors and show them just what it is that you are achieving in your classroom but certainly don't beat yourself up about not mentioning *everything*. Have realistic expectations of yourself and you're most likely to impress inspectors with your daily classroom practice.

I am very concerned that my performance management records will be given to inspectors. Is there a way I can prevent this from happening?

This won't happen, and if it does, you have serious cause for complaint. Your performance management records are (or at least should be) totally confidential and inspectors are told that they should never request them, or accept them if they are offered, unless it is impossible to identify who they belong to.

How relevant is the work that schools do to promote community cohesion when it comes to Ofsted inspection?

It is very relevant, particularly as Ofsted has been reporting on the contribution made by schools to promoting community cohesion since September 2008. This means that it really is important to show and tell inspectors exactly how you contribute to this in your school and specifically in your classroom. The Education and Inspections Act 2006 introduced the duty on all schools to promote community cohesion so this should already be a pretty strong feature of what your school does. Basically, this kind of cohesion means that pupils can be helped to appreciate others from different backgrounds, to develop a sense of shared values and to feel a part of a community in which they will be able to enjoy and achieve.

Alan Johnson, Secretary of State for Education and Skills, speaking to Parliament on 2 November 2006, defined community cohesion as meaning:

> working towards a society in which there is a **common vision** and **sense of belonging** by all communities; a society in which the diversity of people's backgrounds and circumstances is appreciated and valued; a society in which similar **life opportunities** are available to all; and a society in which strong and positive relationships exist and continue to be developed in the workplace, in schools and in the wider community.

(Johnson's speech referred to the government's and the Local Government Association's definition first published in *Guidance on Community Cohesion*, LGA, 2002, and resulting from the Cantle Report in 2001.)

The following ideas may help enhance your preparedness for inspection regarding this important dimension of school life:

- Does your school work with an international partner school? This is a great way of enhancing cohesion and of focusing on Britain's identity. If your school doesn't have an international twin, think about the ways in which you achieve this cohesion during the course of your work in the classroom. See below for information on the Global Gateway.
- Aim to pick out on lesson plans the features of your lessons which promote community cohesion. A good place to start with this is through discussion and debate.
- Demonstrate how you remove any barriers to learning which may exist. How do you promote cohesion by promoting access for all?
- How do you encourage children and their parents and families to interact with each other regardless of background? This all feeds into community cohesion.
- Do you reach out into your local community at all? What about links with schools in your family group? Show inspectors how this helps to promote community cohesion.
- Be explicit about the areas of the curriculum where you promote common values and encourage children to value differences and combat prejudice.
- What visits do you organise which also help to promote community cohesion?
- How about the support you offer for pupils who speak English as a second or other language?
- Think about the way in which your school approaches incidents of bullying and harassment. Is there a clear community cohesion dimension to this? How about the way in which you as an individual deal with such incidents when they occur in your classroom? Can you add the phrase 'community cohesion' to any bullying policies?

- In what ways do you, as an individual teacher, work with community representatives, local agencies and parents? Is community cohesion a natural by-product of any of these activities?
- Do you know exactly how you, or your school, would deal with any incidents of racial discrimination?
- Can you identify what the barriers to community cohesion in your school might be? This isn't about highlighting what's wrong, but rather about finding what might be improved and showing inspectors just what you have achieved in the pursuit of community cohesion! Barriers to cohesion typically come in the form of mistrust of difference, a sense of unfairness in the way in which different groups are treated and a lack of opportunity for people from different backgrounds to interact and learn from one another.
- How, precisely, do you blast through intolerances of any kind in your classroom? Be mindful of the opportunities to promote community cohesion which exist in your handling of such situations.
- Do your pupils appreciate the various tiers of community of which they are a part? For example, they are part of their school community, the local community in which the school is located, the UK as a national community and the global community.
- Are equality of opportunity and inclusion features of your lesson planning?
- In what ways do the Every Child Matters outcomes (see below) feed into your promotion of community cohesion and vice versa?
- The legislation that is relevant to community cohesion includes: the Equality Act 2006; the Race Relations (Amendment) Act 2000; and the Children Act 2004. Aim to gain some insights into the ways in which these can influence our work in the classroom.

The above is intended to provide you with just some starting points in your consideration of this important feature of school life. It has been said before but it's worth stressing again: it's essential to make explicit to inspectors what is implicit in your work. Don't ever assume that inspectors will pick up the finer details of what you achieve in the classroom. They may do, but unless you show them, you can never be sure. You can find out more about enhancing community cohesion from the Teachernet website (see below).

Find out more ...

- For further information on professional learning teams visit the website of the National College for School Leadership: www.ncsl.ac.uk
- To access Ofsted reports on the Ofsted website visit www.ofsted.gov.uk. If you go to the homepage and click on 'Inspection reports' you will find a search facility.
- The Teachernet website can be accessed via: www.teachernet.gov.uk
- Information on the Every Child Matters Agenda can be found on the website: www.everychildmatters.gov.uk
- The Global Gateway to educational partnerships between schools and colleges across the world can be accessed via: www.globalgateway.org.uk
- *Using the Evaluation Schedule: Guidance for Inspectors of Schools* is available to download from the Ofsted website: www.ofsted.gov.uk

CHAPTER 4

Inspection and your well-being

For every time in stress, you need a recovering time in relaxation.
Emmett E. Miller, MD

Introduction

Our well-being is arguably *the* most important consideration at work. Without it, we are not in a position to nurture and support the well-being of the young people in our care and without that, how can they learn? This may be a simplistic approach to the issue of well-being. But in schools where its importance is underplayed, both staff and pupils typically suffer.

Waiting for others to notice our well-being needs is usually a mistake! Taking care of those needs for ourselves is what will improve our resilience and self-reliance and in the long run enable us to support others in their pursuit of well-being. Self-knowledge is the goal, and the great thing about a job like teaching is that it offers ample opportunity to learn about yourself and the way in which you respond to the events and situations it presents you with.

This chapter explores ideas around:

- stress and the concept of inspection
- preventing stress from taking hold
- the symptoms of negative stress

- minimising stress in schools
- depression
- stress-busting
- anxiety
- food and mood
- sleeping soundly
- safeguarding relationships
- fighting colds.

Is an Ofsted inspection really as stressful as some teachers make out?

There is no doubt that some teachers, and schools in general, experience inspection as an inherently stressful event. Organisations such as the Teacher Support Network and teacher unions frequently deal with concerned teachers who are facing inspection, and it's absolutely right that such concerns should be aired and dealt with. However, inspection doesn't need to be a stressful event. The way in which a school experiences inspection is largely down to the way in which senior leadership teams choose to handle the situation. That lead from the top tends to be disseminated rapidly throughout a school. If the head and his/her immediate team take it in their stride, potential stressors are minimised. Likewise, if you as an individual choose to acknowledge inspection as a necessary and potentially useful dimension of your work as a teacher, you're far less likely to be hit by feelings and symptoms of negative stress.

In short, yes, for some teachers inspection is a stressful event, but for others, it is merely a part of the job. While the reactions of staff around you to an imminent inspection will impact your experience to an extent, always remember that *you* are in charge of your response to this situation and can choose to be positively affected by it. Sometimes this is easier said than done, but the bottom line is that our *thinking* about an event can often determine the way in which we experience it. As a wise man said, your focus is your reality.

I'm trying to avoid stressing out about the inspection but I don't think I'm managing! What can I do?

It's really common for teachers to feel that they should be able to cope with everything, even the relatively rare events in their working lives such as inspection. Sometimes, though, we can't! Sometimes we need extra reassurance that all is well and that if we do our best, we are doing enough. That's perfectly normal, but do remember that there's no *need* to feel stressed out. Try to use these feelings to trigger the drive to take you onwards and upwards.

Give yourself permission to face your feelings of stress. If you had broken your leg, you would accept that you could not drive while it was encased in plaster – you would not give yourself a hard time over having to alter your way of being until healing had taken place. The same applies to negative stress. If a day off would help, take it. If delegating some basic chores would help, delegate. If a reduction in your workload would help, do all in your power to achieve this (adopt some assertiveness skills, use your powers of persuasion, script what you want to say and be mindful of your body language). Whatever you do, do not add to the expectations you have of yourself; the relationship between workload and negative stress is well known.

Think about organising your workload into timed slots and be very strict about going overtime. Take a while to analyse whether you are wasting or leaking time. Can you be more productive and creative in your use of time? Review what you can drop from your 'to do' list. Make plenty of sleep a priority (see below) and put as many non-urgent tasks or events as possible on hold to facilitate this. This applies to tasks in any aspect of your life.

Aim to identify the quiet times in your day. Take the time to look out of the window for a minute or two or sit in an empty room for a while during your lunch break. Drive to and from work in silence. In short, be aware of those moments of quiet stillness which can litter your day. Watch your movements; aim to walk more slowly and be conscious of stilling your mind regularly. And treat yourself! Book yourself a day of doing nothing work-related; whatever it is that does it for you, give yourself the time.

I really feel as though I may be suffering from stress but, funny as it may sound, I'm really not sure! I sometimes feel quite detached and as though I'm going through the motions. What are the symptoms of negative stress that I should be looking out for?

Recognising the symptoms of negative stress is a major step towards eliminating its negative effects. It's very common, though, for people to misinterpret the feelings of stress that they may be experiencing or to put them down to something else entirely. The problem is that the more stressed we get, the less able we are to think clearly about taking action to deal with it. It can be a vicious circle!

It is difficult to identify exactly what symptoms can be attributed to negative stress, simply because they may be physical, emotional or behavioural. If you think that you may be suffering from negative stress, consider these questions:

- What do others say about you? How are you described by your colleagues, friends and family?
- How do others interact with you? Are you patient and attentive or snappy and distracted?
- Are you less confident than you used to be? More shy and introspective?
- Is your mood stable and balanced or do you find yourself swinging from contentment to distress in one go?
- Is decision making more difficult than it used to be and 'good quality' concentration a thing of the past? Do you procrastinate?
- Are your thoughts generally positive or negative? Do you have any thoughts of impending doom?
- Do you rely on stimulants more than usual? Has the occasional drink become a daily necessity? Are you comfort eating?
- Has work taken over where leisure once reigned? Once you have completed your work, do you have the energy for a full social life?
- What are your energy levels like? Do you experience the highs and lows of 'adrenaline dependence'?

Having considered these questions, if you suspect that negative stress may be taking hold it is important to take some action to support yourself. You may want to contact the Teacher Support Network (see below) or your union for career-based advice and it would certainly be worth talking to your chosen healthcare provider about your feelings of negative stress.

Some of the physical and mental or emotional signs and symptoms of negative stress that you may be experiencing include:

- vague feelings of ill-health
- headaches
- palpitations (being aware of your heartbeat)
- dry mouth due to decreased saliva production
- fatigue
- chemical dependence
- digestive problems
- menstrual disturbances
- weight loss or gain (most commonly loss)
- skin problems such as acne and eczema
- raised blood pressure and heart rate
- increased susceptibility to minor infections
- increased sweating
- grinding teeth
- shallow, rapid breathing
- tension in arms and legs
- memory problems
- noise sensitivity
- lack of joy, frequent crying, emotional outbursts
- hopelessness and helplessness
- depression
- preoccupation, perhaps with worrying thoughts
- inability to control anger
- difficulty in being alone
- nightmares
- feelings of dissatisfaction in personal work performance
- loss of confidence, self-worth and self-esteem
- irritability.

Do make sure that you consult your healthcare provider, such as your GP, if you are regularly experiencing any of these symptoms. It's always better to be extra cautious than to ignore your body's clear signals that all is not well.

I'm in a position to influence the way in which my school experiences the inspection. What can I do to help ensure that the process is as positive as possible?

Many schools have devised ways of supporting staff through the general stresses of their jobs, not least at inspection time. The following methods do seem to be particularly effective and you may want to incorporate some of them into your work in this regard:

- Providing written material on effective methods of stress busting within the context of your particular school.
- Facilitating ongoing discussions on the impact on work of the stresses felt by staff in your school.
- Organising peer support groups.
- Providing or facilitating confidential counselling services.
- Arranging visits from therapists with expertise in stress reduction such as reflexologists, yoga instructors, meditation/relaxation instructors and so on.
- Active maintenance of a collective sense of humour! Laughter is an incredibly powerful de-stressor, not least because it is as opposite to the stress response as it is possible to get. There's no way that we can feel stressed and laugh at the same time. If you want to reduce stress, laugh more!
- Modelling appreciation. The more that staff members openly appreciate each other, the less likely it is that negative stress will take hold. When we ignore our colleagues, or fail to recognise their contributions, we're nurturing despondency, therefore creating a rich environment in which stress can thrive. This is particularly important with regard to manager-on-subordinate relationships.

In schools which actively seek to address the stress felt by staff members there seems to be an understanding that regardless of which staff are suffering from negative stress, the impact can potentially affect everyone. In other words, there is a holistic approach to the issue.

Helping others through their stresses is also known to be a great way of helping yourself. It can assist in the search for meaning (and if Nietzsche is to be believed, we can suffer almost any *how* if we can identify a *why*) and it helps us to appreciate just how resilient we are, and just what degree of self-mastery we have. There is no doubt that the chance to serve others is also an incredibly powerful personal development tool: one which is worth utilising as frequently as possible. You can find out more about the concept of 'meaning making' from Viktor Frankl's classic book, *Man's Search for Meaning* (see below).

I suspect that I may be suffering from depression, and my reaction to this inspection just confirms my suspicions. I don't know what to do, and I dread it affecting my work if I go to my GP about it. What should be my next step?

Recognising feelings of depression is a very significant step. It's easy to squash such feelings down and not air them out of fear. But to acknowledge what you are feelings and actively seek a resolution is a brave and ultimately self-supporting thing to do. Stress, anxiety and depression can appear to be very closely linked and concern about their relationship with suicide is growing. It is generally understood that prolonged negative stress can contribute to mental illness and even to psychiatric injury, which can lead to a heightened potential for suicide in susceptible people. One particularly vulnerable group is teachers in their twenties and thirties with a limited social circle (due to work commitments and not having a family of their own) with no close friends or family around them to give them a sense of perspective.

If you feel that you are experiencing depressive thoughts or worse, it is really important to talk to someone about how you are feeling. As soon as you have divulged even a little of the immense emotion inside, you will create the space to start thinking creatively about solutions. But don't attempt this alone. There are always people with expertise to help you. Don't ever feel that you have to tackle this alone. If you are not happy speaking to family and friends, see your GP or other healthcare provider, or speak to the Samaritans or a counsellor from the Teacher Support Network (see below).

It's also a very good idea to talk to those closest to you about how you are feeling. Ask them to keep an eye on you. There are always answers; you do not have to suffer alone indefinitely, but you do need to verbalise your feelings to someone in a position to facilitate hope and help. Answers may come in the form of talking therapies, drugs or complementary and alternative therapies. Increased exercise and an improved diet may also boost mood: the possibilities are many, but you are unique, and worth taking care of.

I need some top tips for stress-busting. What's known to work well?

The key thing to remember when it comes to stress-busting is that you are unique and there is no foolproof formula that's going to set you back in balance every time. The way in which you respond to life will vary depending on what's going on for you, how resilient you feel, how physically fit you are and so on. This ultimately means that your stress-busting toolkit needs to be able to respond to your changing needs. That said, these ideas are known to be useful in combating negative stress:

- Mind/body techniques such as visualisation, meditation, relaxation, t'ai chi, yoga, and so on, are known to impact negative stress. The best way of learning such techniques is to join a class (your local sports, leisure or adult education centre will almost certainly run such courses). However, this might not be practical if your stress has a habit of expressing itself at your busiest times! If you feel unable to join a class, try one of the excellent books on the subject. A browse through a good high street bookshop or an online store such as Amazon will help. It is a good idea to join such a class when your need for positive results is less urgent. That way you are free to learn what it can offer you and apply the skills on a daily basis, but especially when your stress levels rise.

- Develop and nurture a hobby, preferably a creative or sporty one. Once again, if you invest time in the pursuit of a hobby when you are not particularly stressed, you will be more likely to retain the habit, and reap the rewards, when your stress levels rise. As Hal Falvey said, 'a hobby puts to work those unused talents which might otherwise become restless, and it provides us with a form of activity in which there is no need whatever to strive for success.' This complete detachment from any form of success criteria is what offers us respite. We can pursue the hobby for the sake of it and not be assessed, or held accountable in any way. Liberating isn't it?
- If you can feel stress levels rising, stop. Take deep breaths and ask yourself why this is happening. Sometimes the moment at which we identify ourselves as feeling stressed does not relate to the actual stressor. This is usually why we may find ourselves snapping at loved ones or responding harshly to strangers when they are not the source of our angst. It's easy to do, and everyone does it at some stage or other, but best avoided if at all possible. Aim to identify the actual cause of the stress and be specific. What, exactly, was the trigger? What can you do about this now? Go for creative, solution-driven approaches to your stress. And good for you for acknowledging it. That's at least half the battle!
- Become self-observant. When you feel stressed, what are the changes that take place in your body and mind? How positive is your self-talk? Learn to recognise these symptoms as messages from your body. If your back starts to ache when stress takes hold, take action at the first twinge – and better still, anticipate what makes the twinges start and take action before the symptoms have the chance to express themselves physically. Remember that physical symptoms are often your body's final shout that it is not happy with what you are putting it through. If you quieten your mind you will be able to hear its pleas when it is still whispering!
- Find out what soothes you (a book, a particular food, exercise, a certain person or a form of relaxation, for instance).

- Be watchful of those around you. Is anyone dragging you down with his or her persistent negativity? Avoid them as much as possible (unless you want to help them see more positive vistas!).
- Do not seek to attribute blame for the way that you are feeling. Stress and its associated emotions often carry the related underlying sense of not being valued. Of course there is a societal need to value teachers, but no one can make you *feel* valued. That is down to you, just like managing your stress can only be down to you.
- Take care over your diet and intake of chemicals and stimulants such as nicotine, caffeine, alcohol and drugs. Be particularly aware of the fine line that divides social and addictive drinking and watch out for any changes in your drinking habits. Be honest with yourself. That doesn't mean that you have to abstain, but it is important to recognise when a coping mechanism becomes a dangerous habit.
- Seek appropriate professional help as early as possible. The Teacher Support Network is a good place to start and counsellors will be able to identify what or who would be best placed to offer you assistance. Recognise the resources you have inside you to take the step of seeking help.
- Do not underestimate the escapist qualities of books and music. Burying yourself in either for as little as 15 minutes can be incredibly refreshing.
- Stay in the present. Divided attention leads to tension. Focus on each matter in hand and it's far harder to become stressed by life. Allow your mind to leap from one task to the next, while denying yourself the chance to complete anything satisfactorily, and you're almost certain to end up stressed out and feeling useless.

Anxiety is a real problem for me. How can I reduce the amount of anxiety that I feel?

There's a quote from Ovid's writing which goes: 'Happy is the man who has broken the chains which hurt the mind, and has given up worrying once and for all'. There's a sound point in there; just think how free you would feel to have worry and anxiety banished from your life!

There comes a point when excessive negative stress can develop into a full-blown anxiety disorder. Concern about an event such as an inspection, whether it is likely, expected or recently passed, can in a minority of people escalate until anxiety inhibits normal functioning. This in turn leads to stress and so the cycle is perpetuated. Although this is relatively rare (there is some evidence for genetic predisposition to anxiety), and most teachers do not develop anxiety disorders, it is very important to know what the warning signs may be. If this is an issue for you, seek the help of your chosen healthcare provider, such as your GP, sooner rather than later, before the situation deteriorates, especially as what some sufferers believe to be anxiety may in fact be depression.

We do not have that much control over the arrival of fear and anxiety as emotions. Fear certainly has its uses as it can protect us from danger, but when it becomes subjective, problems can arise. Fear and anxiety in connection with an inspection are, by definition, subjective. No one can know in advance what the dynamics between inspectors and your school will be, nor what the outcome of the inspection will be, despite the fact that self-evaluation gives us a very good idea. There has to be an element of 'taking the plunge' and going forward into the inspection with determination so that anxiety about the unknown does not control your response to the situation.

Do keep in mind that fear and anxiety in response to inspection are more likely if you are suspicious of the procedures and what might happen. Use the earlier chapters in this book to become as familiar as possible with the process. It is not designed to trip you up.

There is nothing strange or unusual about self-doubt. Which professional has not experienced some element of self-doubt at some stage? We could go as far as saying that, without it, we're missing a vital opportunity for personal and professional development. However, if this self-doubt becomes excessive, unrealistic or out of all proportion, or if it begins to paralyse you into inaction, expert help is needed. Embrace the possibility that when it comes to inspection, you cannot lose. If high praise emerges from it, allow yourself to feel satisfaction and fulfilment in your work, in the knowledge that you are enabling children to enjoy and achieve. If development needs emerge, move willingly towards making the necessary improvements *while* allowing yourself to feel satisfaction in your developing skills. None of this needs to define you in any way. Your biography is not your identity!

There are both mental and physical symptoms of anxiety to watch out for and if you find yourself experiencing any of those listed below, do seek professional advice (for example, from your GP). The following symptoms may be felt to a greater or lesser degree:

- racing heartbeat
- breathing difficulties, hyperventilation
- dizziness or light-headedness
- nausea
- increased or excessive sweating
- temperature fluctuations
- pins and needles
- menstrual and digestive disorders
- restlessness
- fatigue
- insomnia
- muscle tension
- diminishing concentration
- terror or a feeling of impending doom
- fear of losing control or sanity
- loss of self-esteem
- preoccupation with health
- low mood.

It's not always helpful to 'cope' with anxiety. By 'coping' you may inadvertently accommodate the anxiety, making room for it in your daily routines. The better aim would be to resolve thc anxiety so that both physical and mental symptoms recede, helping to minimise the chances of a recurrence.

Resolving anxiety can be a difficult journey as, in most cases, there will be several contributing factors at its root. That said, with the help of a trusted healthcare provider such as your GP, it is not a mission impossible.

If you find that your anxiety is not abating and may even be tipping into panic, then there is an urgent need to address the key causes (there will invariably be more than one cause). There are many sources of help for this problem, so don't ever feel that you have to face it alone.

Within your school, trusted friends on the staff may offer their support, as may the person with responsibilities for staff well-being. There is no one within a school community that does not have anyone to turn to for advice. Even headteachers can look to colleagues and governors or the local authority.

Outside your school, your local authority or union may have a confidential stress counselling line and there is always Teacher Support Network (see below). Family members and friends may be a source of unparalleled support too. Your healthcare provider will have seen numerous cases of anxiety and panic and will probably have extensive experience of facilitating solutions. You're far from being alone.

If you suspect that what you are experiencing is anxiety or even panic, these points may be helpful:

- The way that you are feeling is not abnormal. It is merely an exaggerated response that can be tamed.
- As long as you address any panic you may experience, long-term harm is highly unlikely; in fact, you will probably learn more about yourself through such experiences than you had thought possible!
- However difficult it may seem, try not to add to your panic by thinking about other things that could possibly go wrong. This can be a challenge, but in a negative state of mind it is easy to slip into thoughts of intractable doom.
- Stay as much as you can with what is happening in the present moment. At this precise moment, as you read these words, all is well. Don't stray into what may or may not happen in the future. Stick with the now!
- Allow your panic to wash over you when it arises. This will help you to understand that it is a temporary situation that will pass. If you are at school, do all you can to get some time alone or in a quiet room, even if it is only for ten minutes or so. The aim is to reduce the amount of stimulation around you. Some people who experi-

ence panic find it is helpful to focus on something *outside* yourself as you breathe deeply to restore balance. For example, look at a picture, a flower, a distant view from a window or something similar.

- Pay attention to your breathing. The deeper you can breathe the faster you will return to a sense of calm and balance. There is only so far that panic can go in a body that is breathing calmly and deeply! Breathing into a hand cupped over your mouth and nose will also allow you to re-breathe some of the carbon dioxide gas you have exhaled. Extend this calm to your movements; walk in a measured way and avoid the need to rush if at all possible.
- A great relaxation exercise is to relax your jaw by unclenching your teeth, placing your lips lightly together and your teeth slightly apart. It is virtually impossible to retain tension in your face in this position. Then start 4-2-4-2 breathing: breathe in to a count of four, hold for a count of two, and then breathe out to a count of four. Keep going until feelings of panic and anxiety recede.
- After an episode of panic, spend time focusing on everything you have achieved in the past. What is *really* blocking your success this time?
- Once the feelings of panic have receded, complete a task that you know will be successful, however small that may be.
- Affirm to yourself that there is plenty of time to complete all you have to complete. You could even construct a panic-busting affirmation that you repeat regularly to yourself throughout the day. For example: 'I am calm and balanced'. Anticipating work not yet done simply leads to weariness and despondency!
- Know that you will handle anything that might arise before, during and after an inspection. Nothing terrible will happen. In fact, your confidence and self-esteem will probably blossom.
- Check yourself when you say 'what if'. This is a blind line of enquiry if ever there was one.
- If you have not enjoyed inspection in the past, do not relive those experiences in anticipation of what is to come. No two inspections are the same. Remember that, often, what we perceive is happening and what is *actually* happening are two completely different things.
- Regular peer observation kills fear. If anxiety has become an issue with you, get someone into your lessons quickly to help give you

some perspective through their observations. Seek out colleagues who support positivity, and be mindful of the influence that others can have on your approach to inspection generally.
- Treat yourself with respect. Think how you would deal with the situation if a child came to you with growing anxieties. Would you treat that child with impatience or with compassion and concern?

So, in brief:

- your feelings are not abnormal
- address your panic
- do not add to your panic
- stay in the present moment
- do not resist your panic
- pay attention to your breathing
- focus on your achievements
- complete a small, easy task
- know that you *will* handle it
- do not say 'what if…'
- view each inspection with fresh eyes
- ask for lesson observations
- respect yourself.

One final word about panic. Panic attacks must be treated very seriously. They are one of the strongest signals your body can give you that negative stress has taken hold. The symptoms of a panic attack can be so severe that the sufferer may mistake them for a heart attack.

Panic attacks usually include shortness of breath, palpitations, sweating, chest pain and a feeling of certain impending doom, often occurring suddenly and without warning. They are perfectly treatable, but on no account should they be ignored. If you suspect that you have suffered a panic attack, seek the advice of your chosen healthcare provider without delay.

Evidence is mounting on the success of flower remedies in helping people to overcome panic attacks. Try Bach Rescue Remedy as a useful support to other treatments you may be pursuing.

I've heard about the impact that food can have on mood, but is there anything I should be doing to make sure that I am as fit for inspection, and work in general, as possible?

The food that you eat can have a very significant impact on your mood and concentration levels and for this reason it's well worth taking a good look at your diet and any supplements you take to make sure that you're giving yourself the best chance of success. One word of caution: it is almost always advisable to consult a qualified nutritionist before starting to supplement your diet with any vitamins, herbs or minerals. While it's usually highly unlikely that you will do yourself any harm through self-prescribing, it is better to know from a professional exactly what it is you should be taking and in what doses. 'Mopping up the floor before turning off the tap' is something to avoid, but at least taking a good look at diet and nutrition generally might put you in a position to tackle the broader picture of what's stressing you.

Mind, the mental health charity (see below), has done a lot of research into the impact of what we eat on our mental and emotional health. There is a developing body of scientific evidence to back this connection up and a mountain of anecdotal evidence. In association with Amanda Geary, the Mind Meal was devised, with the aim of providing people with a simple recipe for a meal with the potential to lift your mood! The meal consists of wheat-free pasta with pesto sauce and oil-rich fish, avocado salad and seeds and a fruit and oatcake dessert. Unfortunately there isn't a vegetarian substitute for the fish, but protein-rich foods such as beans, quorn or tofu chunks can be used and a linseed (flaxseed) or hempseed oil supplement can be taken in addition. You can find the recipe for the Mind Meal on the Food and Mood website (see below).

Do avoid any drastic changes to your diet as this can simply add to any stresses that you may be experiencing. And don't cut back on fat too much either. Your brain is, believe it or not, over 60% fat so going for an extremely low fat diet has the potential of really affecting your mood, leading to depression and anxiety and a whole host of other mental health problems. Omega 3 and 6 essential fatty acids are the ones to go for, found in oily fish and nuts and seeds. You may want to look into this deeper and Amanda Geary's *Food and Mood Handbook* (see below) is a great place to start.

Other supplements that you may find useful in combating stress include:

- Ginseng: this may have memory-boosting properties.
- *Ginkgo biloba*: this may help to improve circulation in the brain and therefore support concentration.
- The B vitamins: these have been found to support the nervous system and are useful to take at times of extra stress. It is advisable to take these in the morning as there is a possibility they may interfere with sleep if taken later in the day.
- Magnesium: it seems that the body can become depleted of this essential mineral when it is under strain. Supplements can be a useful support at times of stress.
- Aromatherapy can be an effective de-stressor for some. Remember to use essential oils safely by diluting them in carrier oils. You can use them in a burner or by adding a few drops to a bath or massage oil. It's thought that ylang-ylang is good for creating a sense of peace while lavender and bergamot are thought to have sedative qualities. Clary sage may have a positive impact on feelings of depression and despondency.
- Bach Flower Remedies are also thought to be gentle but effective in soothing nerves. In particular, Rescue Remedy may have a beneficial calming effect.

I'm not a great sleeper and I know that I will find it difficult to get adequate sleep when we have the inspection. How can I maximise my chances of a good night's sleep at least the night before inspectors arrive?

The importance of a good night's sleep cannot be over-emphasised and yet it can be so difficult to achieve. The desire for sleep can also become what Viktor Frankl would call a 'hyper-intention'. In other words, the more we strive for it, the less able we are to achieve it.

One of the most common causes of insomnia is stress; yet ironically, it is when we are under perceived stress that the restful state of unconsciousness that sleep offers is most needed. Not only does sleep refresh us for a new day, but when the body is asleep its cell damage is repaired and immune function is at its most active.

Increased health niggles and concerns such as colds and coughs seem to be an inevitable consequence of lack of sleep which in turn impacts day-to-day functioning. On top of this, when tiredness takes hold, everything seems so personal; every comment heard can feel like a put-down, and it can seem that the rational mind has gone absent without leave. So much of our well-being hinges on good quality, uninterrupted sleep.

It takes commitment to improve your sleeping patterns, but these ideas will help:

- Camomile tea before bed to ward off insomnia may be an old folk remedy, but there are many who wouldn't be without it. Studies have shown that camomile contains compounds with calming actions.
- Caffeine is most often consumed in greater quantities when under stress but its adrenaline-mimicking qualities lead to an increase in nervous tension, thus exacerbating the problem. Opt for caffeine-free drinks where possible, but if you have a long history of caffeine dependency do not expect to reduce consumption without withdrawal symptoms. Caffeine is addictive, so cutting back slowly is the wisest way.
- Take time to unwind before going to bed, even if only for fifteen minutes. Working late simply borrows time from the next day. Avoid news programmes during the evening; you may even want to try a 'news fast' to see if it relaxes you and facilitates better sleep.
- Aim to regulate your bedtime so that your body gets into the habit of sleep. Go for more hours of sleep before midnight if you possibly can.
- Do not spend hours in bed being unable to sleep. Try getting up (but resist the urge to work) and perhaps do some light reading to bring sleep on.
- Always seek the advice of your chosen healthcare provider if sleeplessness becomes a habit. Sometimes it's necessary to break the cycle and there are a number of treatments you may be offered.

I've just been through an inspection and with hindsight I can see how I allowed it to dominate my life for a short while. This affected my relationship with my partner. How can I guard against that for future inspections?

There is no doubt that being involved in 'special' work projects, such as an inspection, will have a knock-on effect on those you live with. During the research for this book several headteachers and classroom teachers made the comment that those about to undergo inspection should warn their significant others that they may be distracted by the process when it takes place! By asking for support in advance in this way, at least in the short term, you avoid the risk of taking it when it isn't necessarily being given. It can be easy to exhaust the patience of those you live with if you don't communicate why you are perhaps a little more tense than usual. Friends, family and significant others are far more likely to offer practical assistance if they know in advance what is going on for you and how you might be affected. There is a work–home interface that can too often become blurred to the point of being unrecognisable for some teachers. Much of this may seem obvious, but it is still an area of difficulty that conscientious teachers grapple with.

I seem to catch colds very easily and I expect that when we get notice of an inspection, I'll probably succumb. What can I do to ensure this doesn't happen, or if it does, ensure that it is short-lived?

A simple fact of life is that when we are under pressure at work our immune systems take a battering. The evidence of this is the frequency with which people succumb to the common cold. While most doctors would say that a cold lasts a week if you treat it and seven days if you don't (and it's certainly no good asking for antibiotics – they won't work!), there are a few steps you can take that will ease your suffering and perhaps help to prevent a recurrence. Try all these at the first sign of congestion:

- Take relatively high doses of a good quality vitamin C (the jury is out on whether this truly helps but it is worth acknowledging the fact that questions have been asked of the motivations of those who dismiss the taking of supplements as a waste of money). Always seek the advice of a qualified nutritionist when seeking to supplement your diet.

- Suck a zinc lozenge; zinc is thought to reduce the length of time that you are sick.
- Eat lightly (as much fresh raw food as possible) and drink plenty of water. If you are not a natural water drinker try drinking it hot with a teaspoonful of honey in it and/or a squeeze of lemon juice. This is soothing and easy for your body to handle.
- Use eucalyptus essential oil to clear sinuses (put a couple of drops on a tissue and inhale).
- Take time off sooner rather than later if a cold takes hold. Give yourself a chance to get better and you'll find that you are almost certainly stronger when the next round of bugs hits.

Find out more ...

- Teacher Support Network: www.teachersupport.info/
- *Man's Search for Meaning* by Viktor Frankl, Rider Books, 2004, ISBN 9781844132393
- The Samaritans can be reached in a number of ways: **online** at www.samaritans.org; by **email** – jo@samaritans.org; by **post** – Chris, PO Box 9090, Stirling FK8 2SA; or by **phone** – 08457 909090
- *The Food and Mood Handbook* by Amanda Geary, Thorsons, 2001, ISBN 0007114230
- There is also a website dedicated to food and mood: www.foodandmood.org/
- Mind, the mental health charity, can be reached via: www.mind.org.uk. It runs an information line Monday–Friday 09.15 to 17.15: 0845 766 0163.

CHAPTER 5

The effects of inspection on the individual

> Take rest; a field that has rested gives a bountiful crop.
>
> Ovid

Introduction

Inspection is an inevitable part of life as a teacher; we have established that. Regardless of how we interpret the political drivers behind it, the simple fact still remains that it happens and that we must deal with it in the most effective and productive way possible. Inspection *does* impact teachers, some more negatively than others. The key challenge for us is to seize the opportunity to ensure that the process of inspection leaves us *better off* than we previously were. It's an achievable challenge!

This chapter explores ideas around:

- high expectations
- accountability
- facing 'criticism'
- boosting morale
- workplace bullying
- interacting with inspectors.

I feel the burden of high expectations on me. I know that my school will be inspected sooner rather than later, but I've already been told by my head that he expects 'great things' from me! How can I handle expectations better generally?

As Charlie Brown once said, there is no heavier burden than a great potential! Being the 'golden' boy or girl on a team of staff can be great cause for anxiety when an inspection looms. What if inspectors don't share the same views? What if the dynamics of your school are altered as a result of the inspection? What if you go to pieces? These are all destabilising thoughts and concerns which don't serve teachers well when it comes to the all-important job of teaching and learning.

Great expectations can be burdensome, but worrying about them will not ease your path through an inspection. If you feel that you are not living up to the expectations you suspect exist, don't beat yourself up about it. All you can ever be expected to do is your best with the time and resources that are available to you. Whether you crumble under this perceived pressure is up to you, but one thing is (almost) certain: if you do go to pieces you won't fall apart! Don't allow the absorption of unrealistic expectations to ruin your experience of inspection and the potential professional and personal development that can be gleaned from it.

I feel as though the whole concept of inspection is highlighting my accountability and I find this quite paralysing. Is there a better way to be thinking about this so I don't feel quite so overwhelmed?

There's no doubt that accountability is a crucially important dimension of the job of being a teacher. While it's absolutely right that the role should be accountable, it's very difficult to determine to whom and to what teachers are actually accountable. School leaders, governors, parents, local authorities, inspectors, pupils, society as a whole, governments and so on all demand the attention of teachers and this creates potential conflicts of interest and stress points where

there needn't be any. In addition, the whole con
seems to have a symbolic meaning which is q
literal meaning and it's this symbolism which has
lyse even the most conscientious of teachers. Pe
The teachers who suffer most as a result of t
to view the notion of accountability as a regula
other words, something which has to be externa
for them to perform their duties and roles to ac
This is always a self-defeating trap.

Aim not to think about accountability as a reason t
tice in the classroom defensively. This isn't necessary at
not what Ofsted inspection is all about. A more positi
think of accountability as a driver to providing clarity an
your work for the benefit of all those you are working f

When it comes to inspection, keep it simple. Don't g
by the sheer potential scope of accountability, but rathe
your school and its pupils. It doesn't have to be compl
what you've always done, to the best of your ability and
with the policies and guidance of your school and you wi
every obligation to be accountable. Remember: keep it sir

There's a quote which goes: 'criticism is hard to tak particularly from a relative, a friend, an acquaintan or a stranger'. That's exactly how I feel! How can I b more open to the views of inspectors when they visit school?

For some teachers their view of Ofsted inspection is that it
finding exercise. This only serves to make the process of rece
feedback which might be deemed 'critical' even more tortu
problematic than it might be. By cringing at the thought of c
you're shattering the chances of the whole inspection exercise
you the opportunity to participate in teaching actively, as a
professional. And to top it all, inspectors shouldn't be 'criticising
their purpose is to identify what a school does well and what it
usefully work on for the good of the pupils.

and able to develop as a professional is by fa
forward. And who wants blind, possibly ru
Just a quick word about unfair criticism:
of many a pupil too! Don't ever feel that yo
back given to you, particularly during the
what's known as taking an active role and
Above all else, view your inspection with
Pessimism cannot serve you well and will
about what it is in your job that you do rea
your job and what you are looking forwa
There are no intractable problems when i

I feel as though I need to boost my it's an over-reaction, but the thoug isn't going down very well and I do overshadow the potentially positiv getting from it. What can I do?

It's great to take responsibility for boo
fantastic if your colleagues routinely d
but at especially busy times, we cann
keep our spirits high. Being self-relian
liberating way to be. These ideas may

- Actively seek opportunities to pra
some aspect of their work or yo
the best ways of enhancing your
that of your colleagues. It can be
but the reality is that it's free an
One school actually requested th
encouraging things to other mem
during an inspection but was
continued. *All* staff personnel a
- Never underestimate the posit
amazing ability to mellow the
temporarily), oxygenate the blo

and relax muscles. Many hospitals have collections of humorous writings for patients to read, and research into the positive benefits of laughter is being published thick and fast. In Canada it was found that managers who facilitated the best performance in employees used humour more often than those who were less motivating. Research in California has also found that laughter can strengthen the immune system. Forget the 'inner child'; this is a time for the 'inner comedian'!

- Encourage a sense of balanced perspective in yourself and in others. Inspection, and work in general, does not need to rule your happiness or self-worth. Recognise what you and others can control (such as your responses to situations) and cannot control (such as the fact that inspection does exist). Strive for balance even when emotions are running high, as is inevitable at one stage or another in just about every place of work.
- Music is a great way to ease strains and soothe minds. Either encourage the use of recorded music in your school whenever possible or, as one school did, get a live band and choir together. You may be amazed at the hidden musical talents of your colleagues!
- Be aware of your confidence levels particularly when an inspection is imminent. If you feel them slipping for any reason, you may be more vulnerable to what others say. Just a few words or a look can shatter your esteem at such times, and being conscious of this can prevent what at other times you may see as an over-reaction. Be aware also of the impact of your words on others who may be similarly vulnerable.
- Give yourself and others a treat. It doesn't matter how small the treats are, or how little (if anything) they cost, it's the habit of experiencing something as a treat that can make us feel self-nurtured. It's all in our perception.
- Don't lose sight of life beyond your inspection: it does exist. Arrange something to look forward to and don't pile yourself up with resolutions.
- Be aware of the myths surrounding inspection. For the vast majority of people it is a perfectly positive experience and there's no reason why it can't be for you too.

I am starting to appreciate that I may have been suffering from workplace bullying and now that I am experiencing inspection at my school this is simply confirming the matter for me. What does workplace bullying look like and what are the tell-tale signs that might manifest in me?

Sadly it isn't just pupils who suffer from bullying in schools. In fact, teachers are thought to be among the most likely to suffer from bullying in the workplace (closely followed by healthcare workers) so take comfort from the fact that you are not alone. None of that makes it excusable though, and workplace bullying remains illegal on several counts.

While it would be remiss of a school not to have a policy on how it plans to deal with child-on-child bullying, it still seems that adult-on-adult bullying isn't so carefully considered in schools. This is short-sighted in the extreme. Bullying and stress are closely interrelated so if you are suffering from workplace stress it is essential to determine whether bullying may be an underlying cause.

While everyone has a clear understanding of the kinds of behaviour that constitute bullying between children, there is no clear consensus on what adult-on-adult bullying really is. Within the context of a school, it would be reasonable to define bullying as:

- insidious, relentless criticism (without the offer of constructive, corrective advice);
- humiliation (such as reprimands in front of other staff or pupils);
- excessive work expectations (unrealistic demands prior to or after an inspection);
- abuse of discipline or competency procedures;
- inappropriate forms of communication (shouting, ordering, bombardment via memo or email and so on);
- inexcusable blocks to vital information;
- withholding of recognition for performance;
- manipulation;
- lack of compensation for difficult circumstances.

The impact that bullying involving any of the above can have is likely to be significant. If you can identify that you have suffered from any of the above you may find that you are having to contend with:

- reactive depression
- hyper-vigilance
- shattered confidence
- anxiety
- fatigue
- stress
- digestive disorders
- menstrual disorders.

All of these responses are perfectly natural, and even normal, under the circumstances. Symptoms should be short-lived but only if the source of the bullying is dealt with.

Remember, adult bullies seek to exert power negatively and consistently over another person with the purpose of inciting fear and causing professional and emotional damage. There is inherent destructiveness in the bully, but it should be remembered that his/her actions often result from feelings of inadequacy which are deflected onto another person who may be accused of displaying the very flaws that the bully fears are evident in themselves. Just as children are often bullied because of their positive traits, the same can be true of adult victims who may be seen as being too popular, accomplished or incorruptible, or who highlight others' incompetence through their competence.

There is a clear difference between strong management and bullying. Good managers will have systems in place to detect aspects of the work performance of colleagues that may need correcting and give advice in good time. This is a crucial part of their job. Yet, there are tell-tale signs of bullying-tolerant institutions, indicating that the line between strong and effective management and bullying is frequently crossed. These signs include high absenteeism and turnover of staff, low morale amongst staff and a sub-culture of disrespect of management.

There is more on dealing with workplace bullying in Chapter 8 that you may find useful.

I feel nervous about interacting with inspectors. How can I keep this in perspective?

The first thing to remember is that inspectors are simply doing a job. It might not be a very popular job but they are more than familiar with life in schools and with what it's like for teachers to face inspection. Just treat them like any other human, with a smile and a welcome. (As the Dalai Lama says, it's illogical to expect smiles from others if we aren't prepared to smile ourselves. In other words, many things depend on our own behaviour.)

Building a good relationship with inspectors when they arrive in your school is important and will greatly ease your path through the process, regardless of how little you interact with them. Remember, an inspection should never be done *to* you. You are a crucial part of the process and the relationship between inspectors and the teachers at the schools they inspect must be open to growth on both 'sides'. This means that your input into how it will work best is as valid as an inspector's.

Taking the time to build rapport with inspectors, to put across your character and take a sense of ownership of what happens will help you to influence your experience of inspection. It wouldn't be appropriate to act in a deferential manner towards inspectors. If anything, think of them as professional equals contributing to the delivery of the education service in this country. Just be aware that for many teachers, their professional life draws heavily on the essence of all that is them – their very character and personality. Their style and performance is *them*. If this is the case for you, consider how this could cloud your relationship with inspectors if you feel judged as you the *person* rather than you the *teacher*.

A great deal hangs on the skills of the inspectors in making teachers feel at ease throughout the inspection process but don't absolve yourself of all responsibility here! It is the combination of what teachers and inspectors bring to such relationships that determines its success.

Find out more ...

- You can find out more about the effects of inspection on the individual from your union or from the Teacher Support Network: www.teachersupport.info

CHAPTER 6

Getting ready for inspection

> Human beings, by changing the inner attitudes of their minds, can change the outer aspects of their lives.
>
> William James

Introduction

Getting ready for an inspection is all about the way in which you normally work. Back in the days when schools received long periods of notice of inspection, things were very different, and teachers spent hours on extraordinary preparation. Now, it's much more about developing an everyday preparedness for inspection so that it merely slots into a normal working week. When you receive little or no notice, preparation takes on a whole new meaning!

Most features of preparation for inspection are simply based on sound working practices. There are no tricks or hidden meanings here. Getting ready for Ofsted needn't be an ordeal; in fact it's most effective as a process if inspectors see you as you normally operate, not with bells, whistles and bunting out to celebrate their arrival. Taking an on-going approach to your readiness for inspection is what will serve you best and help you to maintain equilibrium at work and consistently high standards for your pupils. Don't think of inspection as a one-off event which requires your undivided attention. It simply isn't like that. Rather, consider it simply as a time when a team of people visit your school to observe what happens, discuss teaching and learning with staff and pupils and offer their opinion (based on the evidence you provide them with) on what your school is achieving. It's as simple as that.

This chapter explores ideas around:

- creating an Ofsted action plan
- anticipatory stress
- resilience
- assertiveness
- affirmations
- focus on health
- preparing pupils
- top tips for being ready
- preparing resources
- schemes of work.

I have heard that some schools devise Ofsted action plans. How would I go about doing this for myself?

It is true that some schools have Ofsted action plans which are implemented as soon as notice of inspection is given. These plans set out in detail exactly what might be expected to happen in the school in the few days before an inspection starts and the days when inspectors are in school. This level of organisation works well for some leadership teams, and when detailed plans are disseminated around the whole staff, everyone knows what is expected.

If your school is one that has an Ofsted action plan for the event of an inspection, your personal action plan should be linked in directly to it. If your school has not devised one, you may want to consider creating one for yourself along these lines, which would take you through from the moment you hear about the inspection to the end of it:

- Book yourself a treat for the first weekend after the inspection. (Deal with the most important things first.)
- Discuss with your headteacher the possibility of cancelling any off-site visits (that don't involve pupils) or courses that you are due to take part in.

- Take a look at your timetable for the days the inspectors will be in your school. Are there any immediate concerns? If so, discuss these with your line manager or headteacher.
- Complete lesson plans (as usual) for each lesson or session. It is wise to make explicit what might usually be implicit in your lesson planning. In other words, you need to *show* and *tell* the inspectors what normally goes on in your classroom. To this end, make sure that you include reference to those children you teach who have special educational needs, medical needs or who are gifted and talented, and how you intend to utilise any classroom support you have. Every Child Matters, so it is likely that differentiation will be a significant focus of the inspection.
- Make sure that you are fully confident in the knowledge areas you will be teaching during the inspection. This isn't to say that teachers are typically vague about what they teach, but being realistic, we all know that there are some areas we feel stronger about than others. If the inspection happens to fall during a less confident period, it will be worth doing some revision.
- Look into contingency planning. What would you do if there was an emergency, and if, for some reason, you couldn't use your usual room? How will you cope if the technology you are relying on fails, or if the weather affects your plans? Being prepared for all eventualities will substantially ease your experience of inspection.
- If you haven't done so already, identify some examples of work which you consider to demonstrate high, medium and low ability attainment.
- Make sure that marking is up to date and properly recorded.
- Remind yourself which children are looked after, ethnic minority or considered to be at risk.
- Go over any IEPs (provision maps) and make sure that they are in order and accessible to inspectors.
- Check that all the resources you want access to are actually available. Discuss solutions with your line manager if they are not.
- Take a look at any records that you keep to check they are well filed and accessible.
- Cast an eye over your wall displays and general classroom organisation to check that the environment you teach in is an accurate reflection of who you are as a teacher.

- Make sure you are prepared to continue with any pre- or after-school clubs that you run.

This may seem like a daunting plan of action, but really, it is all about being able to engage with inspectors with calm assurance that you are completely on top of your job. Remember, much of this is what you do routinely anyway, but making explicit what's implicit is what inspection is all about.

I've felt stressed about work before and I know what that feels like, but the thought of an inspection is something else! Help!

Calm down; keep it all in perspective. There are very few variables in the process of inspection, but the most significant ones are the behaviour and attitude of inspectors and the way in which the event is perceived in your school. Your school only has total control over one of those variables, and the way in which it responds is likely to be strongly influenced by the attitude of one person: the headteacher. What *you* have complete control over is the way in which *you* choose to respond to inspection. That's not to be taken lightly. It's an incredibly empowering thought to accept responsibility for your reaction to an event such as an inspection and if you're to get the most out of this, for your own benefit and for the benefit of those that you teach and work with, it's essential to view pre-inspection jitters as an *enabling* process. *Use* this anxiety to help you to both show and tell inspectors exactly what a great teacher you are. These ideas may also work for you:

- Act quickly if negative stress and anxiety are in danger of impacting your performance. Don't let things fester or you risk this state becoming the norm for you and this can be devastating.
- Consider the fact that it is possible to become stressed out by *anything*; a visit to the dentist or even crossing the road can carry inordinate amounts of stress for some people. One tried and trusted method of alleviating such stress is to bring the event down to its appropriate size in your mind. Affirm to yourself that it is

only an inspection. This can work surprisingly well. You should also consider where these feelings came from: is inspection the fulfilment of your worst fear? Why? Can you change this belief to one which is more realistic and supportive? Remember, there is absolutely nothing inherently stressful about inspection.

- Inspection, like life, is a temporary situation. *It will pass.*
- Know yourself. If you can pinpoint your skills, strengths and development needs, you are unlikely to be shocked by the verdict of an inspection (regarding your part in it at least). Focus on *your* response to the inspection and distance yourself from the response of others. Some people will want to push through the inspection demanding an inordinate amount of energy from themselves and those around them, while others will relax into it. Carve your own path through the pre-inspection stages and don't be overly influenced by others (unless, of course, they are being supportive).
- Ask more questions about the inspection process if you have any areas of uncertainty. Learn about what will happen within the context of your school so that you can feel prepared.
- Work as hard on your self-esteem and self-worth as you do on any preparation. A solid belief in yourself will serve you far better than a pool of self-doubt. Throw away the 'what ifs' as soon as they enter your mind and replace them with positive affirmations.

I want to approach this inspection with some sense of resilience. What's the best way to achieve this?

Resilience is seemingly under-rated in today's world (or rather, it's not exactly an overt feature of what we teach young people) and yet it is the very core of what makes us able to thrive in our lives. At the heart of resilience is the belief and understanding that we are not alone in the world. There are many sources of connection: for some this comes from spiritual or religious belief, for others it is more centred on being part of society while others may derive it from being part of an extended family. It really doesn't matter what lens you view your connection through. The fact remains that the resilient person allows him- or herself to *feel* a connection and to use this as a driver in life to pursue altruistic urges.

Another feature of resilience is the choice we have to gain from each and every situation we find ourselves faced with. In that respect, resilience may be found in our optimism and courage, in the realistic goals that we set for ourselves, in our self-confidence and self-worth, our creativity and service.

The chances are that you are a naturally optimistic and resilient person. Generally that's what we tend to be, or at least, what we tend towards. But it is worth considering the view that we cannot command ourselves to feel a certain way. A forced optimism or sense of resilience is as beneficial as it is genuine. Rather than *pursue* such states, they *ensue* largely from the meaning we make for ourselves as a result of our reflections on life. In other words, we have a reason to feel that way (just as we laugh when are amused – the amusement is the *reason*).

An inspection is a fantastic opportunity to take stock and *show* another just what you are achieving and are capable of becoming. Treat it as a cause for celebration and an opportunity to shine. That kind of attitude is feeding your well of resilience and will help you to gain as much as possible from the experience.

I'm not the most assertive of people and want some quick workable tips to help me develop these skills. What do you recommend?

Assertiveness is an incredibly valuable tool in any career but especially in the teaching profession. Being assertive is not about being selfish or aggressive, neither is it about being passive. It's a strategy for communication which seeks to be self-supporting and yet respectful of the person you are communicating with. When you are assertive, you express your feelings, opinions and desires in a reasonable and reasoned way which demonstrates that you have listened to the person you are communicating with.

Here are some top tips for developing assertiveness:

- Do not expect people to know what you want or need. It's perfectly reasonable to be as explicit as possible about what you want.

- Do not feel that you are burdening others when expressing yourself. You have a right to be assertive, just as others have a right to express themselves assertively to you.
- If you think you struggle being assertive, try scripting what you want to say in advance. Become a 'broken record' if you have to! Mentally rehearse what you want to convey and visualise what the response may be. Cast yourself in the role of success.
- Be utterly realistic in your goals. If you are asked to do something which you know will tip you over into the realms of negative stress then employ a little bargaining power.
- Pay attention to your body language. Are you giving clues away that you do not fully believe in what you are saying? Is there a conflict between your intention, your desires and your delivery? Aim to be as transparent as possible in your dealings with others.
- Be willing to negotiate and expect positive outcomes.

I've heard that affirmations can be effective at work but have no idea how to use them. Where should I start?

An affirmation is an often-repeated phrase which focuses on something positive. Using affirmations is an excellent way of managing negativity, or those powerful yet crippling moments when confidence shrinks to nothing. There are some points to remember when constructing them:

- Always use positive statements. Say 'My lessons that are observed by inspectors are brilliant' rather than 'There are no problems in the lessons that I teach'.
- Use present rather than future statements: 'The inspection is going very well', rather than 'The inspection will go well'.
- Visualise your ideal scenario when you use affirmations. Believe that you can create the situations you want to create.
- Repeat your affirmations often throughout the day.

I'd like to use my experience of preparing for inspection as a trigger to create a healthy new me at work! How can I focus on this without becoming fanatical about it?

When you're working in such a busy career it's easy to get swamped by the demands of each day and forget to take good care of your health. Add inspection into the mix and, temporarily at least, most of your good intentions fall by the wayside. That's normal, but if you can pay yourself a little attention every now and then, you should minimise any negative impact.

Many schools still report increased levels of sickness in the months following an inspection. It certainly seems that those who are susceptible do struggle to maintain sound levels of health, and the event, which should slip naturally into the normal work of the school, does take its toll. Good health is not a foregone conclusion, and there are no magic recipes for its maintenance. For most people, it is a matter of on-going self-observation in order to maintain balance, remembering that prevention is a more favourable option than cure. The following ideas may appeal to you:

- Ginger tea has been shown to keep the brain alert. Perhaps try some lemon and ginger tea for a boost rather than ordinary tea or coffee if you are in need of an injection of mental energy.
- Take regular exercise, even if it is just brisk walking. It is possible to feel the benefits from as little as ten minutes of focused exercise a day but if you can do more, even better. Choose something that you really enjoy so that you are more likely to keep it up when work pressures fluctuate.
- Teaching is a high energy job and more physically demanding than many outside the profession can imagine. Find out what boosts your energy – perhaps a good quality multi-mineral supplement or a natural therapy treatment – and be conscious of when your energy is waning and needing a lift.
- Evidence is mounting in favour of good quality antioxidants in the battle to prevent illness. By eliminating harmful free radicals in your body, antioxidants play an important role in the maintenance of good health.

- If fatigue is an issue for you, aim to eat at least one raw meal a day. Raw food is said to place fewer demands on the digestive system, leading to more efficient assimilation of nutrients. Eating small amounts regularly throughout the day (sometimes referred to as 'grazing') can also help you to feel more energised, especially if your emphasis is on fresh fruit and vegetables.
- Drink plenty of water. It helps to flush out toxins from the body like no other fluid, and is also extremely effective at keeping headaches at bay if taken regularly throughout the day and certainly at the first sign of pain. Water is such a health-giver; don't underestimate how much better you may feel by committing to drinking more of it regularly through the day.
- If you feel as though your health may be suffering as a result of your work, make a list of your duties and responsibilities that can be carried out temporarily by others. For example, if cooking is usually shared in your household, perhaps you could be given a break until you're back on top. The possibilities are endless, but it's important to ask and discuss these things rather than leave it until you feel overwhelmed. Actively seek the help of others; you will probably be surprised at how keen friends and family members are to help out if you ask in good time.
- Take an immunity-boosting supplement if you feel you are succumbing to bugs and germs more easily than normal. Echinacea, garlic, bee pollen and aloe vera are all thought to be good choices. Your local health store will be able to identify the best one for you, or alternatively consult a qualified practitioner.
- Be mindful of your thinking. There is no doubt (as numerous studies have shown) that optimism and positivity can halt the course of illness and, indeed, help to prevent it from taking hold in the first place. If you respond well to humour, actively seek it out as often as possible; laughter is another reliable health-giver.
- Remember to let your healthcare provider check out any persistent health issues you may have.

Should I prepare my pupils for an inspection in any way? If so, how?

Ofsted inspection still has a relatively high media profile (although not as great as in the past), and for this reason, older pupils at least may well be aware of what is going on in their school, why it is happening, and also that a report on the quality of education being offered to them will soon be in the public domain.

In order to counter-balance this knowledge among pupils, some teachers feel the need to encourage the belief that it is the pupils that are being inspected and not the teachers. By placing responsibility on pupils to perform well for them and for the school as a whole, it is presumably hoped that disruption during any observed lessons will be kept to a minimum. This is probably a bad route to take; if your pupils are sufficiently 'switched on', they will realise that what you tell them is out of fear, rather than out of a genuine concern for their welfare. Naturally the work of a school is achieved through teamwork and pupils are central to that team, but the responsibility for a successful inspection does not lie with them.

Clearly opinion varies on the extent to which pupils should be prepped about the concept of inspection in general, but these points are thought to be useful:

- Depending on their age, stage and level of interest, take time to talk to your pupils about the possibility of inspectors coming to their classroom to observe.
- Take a long-term approach to building sound relationships with the pupils that you teach. This is the best way of helping to ensure cooperation in the event of an inspection!
- Inspectors are likely to move around any classrooms they visit and won't sit in one spot to observe. It can be worth telling pupils that at the start of an inspection so that they know what to expect.
- Explain to pupils that inspectors like to talk to children to find out what it is that they are learning, what they understand, where they have come from in their learning and where they think they are heading, and how it fits into the broader picture of their work in school.

While you cannot know precisely when inspectors will be visiting your school, you can make sure that pupils are generally aware of the answers to these kinds of questions. This is, after all, good practice and will certainly help children to feel empowered in their learning. It also helps to feed into the personalisation agenda too.

- Teach pupils generally about how you would expect them to respond to the questions of visitors to your classroom. This doesn't need to be within the context of inspection, necessarily. The standards you'd expect would be the same regardless of who the visitor is, or where they are from.
- Explain that if an inspector comes to watch what goes on in the room and speaks to any of them individually, he/she may want to write down what they say. Emphasise the need for pupils to feel that they can respond to such questions with complete openness and honesty.
- Some pupils may feel inhibited during class discussions if there is a stranger in the room. Should this be the case during an inspection, explain that it is safe for them to participate and that all the usual rules and routines regarding respectful listening and so on still apply.
- Take the opportunity to re-emphasise respect for each other and for the property in your classroom. This is routine stuff for teachers anyway, and doesn't necessarily need to be linked to an inspection.
- Above all else, don't ever attempt to stage-manage anything for the benefit of inspectors. Most will see through your efforts and invariably even the best laid plans go astray!

When inspectors talk to your pupils they will want to be able to ascertain whether your school listens to their views and the extent to which it acts on them. They will probably also want to ask pupils about the way in which your school handles bullying, racial incidents and poor behaviour as well as asking them about what they consider to be your school's main strengths.

What are the top tips for being ready for an inspection from those in the know?

There is a lot of folklore out there on what works and how schools might improve their general preparedness for inspection. Some of these might work for you:

- Get into the habit of documenting planning in such a way that it could be easily understood by someone who isn't involved in the delivery of lessons. This may only mean subtle changes, if any, to what you do already, but it will be worth the effort.
- Be explicit about the differentiation and personalisation you do and facilitate. For many teachers this is implicit in their daily work anyway, but inspection is all about making crystal clear what it is that you routinely do. Don't assume that anything will be picked up without it being pointed out (of course that happens, but if you want to be *sure* that an inspector has noticed something you have to *tell* them).
- Make sure that individual education plans, behaviour management notes, planning for gifted and talented pupils and so on are well organised and accessible for inspectors.
- Keep displays current and aim to keep a display log and plan for future displays so that if inspectors arrive when your walls aren't their best you can show what they have been and what they are due to become. This is perfectly acceptable.
- Go with the adrenaline buzz that is bound to hit your school when inspectors arrive. You're all in it together and it can be quite exciting.
- Acknowledge the fact that partners and other family members don't always 'get' what inspection is about and the effect it can have on teachers. Talk about what's going on for you, and if necessary ask for some extra consideration. It's all about communication. Don't expect people to *know* what it's like for you. Tell them.
- Have respect for the system. After all, that's what we expect of pupils. If we approach inspection from this perspective it makes it much easier to experience.

- Remember your colleagues. Schools which tend to sail through inspection aim to minimise the isolation that can be felt by teachers. This is not a question of 'every man for himself'. Work as a team.
- Be as familiar as you can with the data your school has. Make sure you've read, and keep up to date with, your school's policies, and take a good look round its website every now and then.
- Make sure you're absolutely clear about the Every Child Matters agenda and how it is played out in your school.
- Get into the habit of developing and maintaining portfolios of evidence of work done, standards achieved and progress made. Pick out examples of excellence and evidence of how rich the curriculum is that you offer.
- Cultivate the attitude that when inspectors arrive, the inspection will be done *with* you rather than *to* you.
- Don't fall into the trap of thinking that you can never do enough; you can.
- Keep a running list of aspects of school life that you can show inspectors when they arrive. For example, if you are involved in the school choir or orchestra, you may want to consider having set pieces ready for demonstration.
- Think about which children you would volunteer to speak to inspectors should you get the chance. This may change over time, but it's worth thinking about this in advance. Children are the best ambassadors for a school, so the more articulate the better. Don't, whatever you do, brief them – inspectors can spot this a mile off.
- Always be mindful of *progress*. That's what floats inspectors' boats! Some teachers even keep a journal of examples of good progress. This is an incredibly useful tool to refer to once inspectors arrive and ask you about the progress that your pupils make. Even if that doesn't happen, it's still an excellent boost to look at as a reminder of what a great job you're doing.
- Get ready to show off your innovations! Be proud and talk highly of everything that is unique and effective about what you are achieving at school.
- Inspectors will want to see children taking responsibility. Create opportunities for this that can then be demonstrated to Ofsted.

- Inspection is all about finding out how good you are as a school. It isn't about tripping you up. Remember that!
- Take advantage of shared observations. The more used you get to having people in your classroom, the easier it will be when inspectors arrive. Get into the habit of watching each other teach. If nothing else, this is an excellent development tool.
- Remember, Ofsted is not the be all and end all! There is a bigger picture; you have a wider dimension to your life. Keep it all in perspective and do the very best you can.

I've heard that I should be preparing amazing resources for the inspection but with such short notice this isn't realistic. What is the best thing to do?

Naturally, when planning lessons that you know might be observed by an inspector, you will want to make sure that any resources that you use are going to impress. There is no problem with this, as long as you aren't staying up all night, honing creative talents you never knew you had or spending a fortune on props that may never see the light of day again. After all, the whole point of the inspection is for inspectors to see you school as it usually operates. They want to see business as usual not a stage-managed extravaganza.

Unless your pupils are either very young or very unobservant, they will quickly give it away if they are not used to lessons so well resourced. It only takes one of them to say that you're only doing it for the benefit of inspectors and your hopes of creating a good impression will deflate quicker than you can say 'performance-related pay'!

It's only natural to want to impress (within reason), but do err on the side of tweaking what you would have been using anyway. The last thing you want is to be so exhausted from your preparations that you don't sparkle in the delivery.

When creating and preparing resources for your lessons, the following ideas may help:

- Make sure that any lesson resources you prepare are not so out of the ordinary that pupils become suspicious!

- Make sure that any resources you plan to use during the inspection do not require inordinate amounts of last-minute preparation or setting up just in case you have an audience! You'll want to be focusing on other things, such as the progress of your pupils.
- Make sure that all your lesson props are in working order. It sounds obvious, but what is permissible in an unobserved lesson may come over as ill-advised when inspectors are in the room, simply because the full context may not be appreciated.
- Make sure that you can relate your use of any resources to your expectations of pupils.
- Aim to have enough resources for any visiting inspectors to have copies (if appropriate).
- Remember that inspectors will be more impressed by basic resources which really add value to your lessons than flashy resources of dubious need.
- Avoid using resources that will fundamentally change the way in which you teach.
- Inspectors may want to look at the quality of resources you have at your disposal, such as textbooks, equipment and apparatus. This will help them to determine how well budgets are deployed throughout your school. For this reason, it is a good idea to ensure that your resource areas are clutter-free and organised so that a quick assessment can be made. Don't forget that the comments in the final report relating to the quality of the resources that you have to work with may result in a boost to your department's or year group's budget. It could even be wise to make it known if you have suffered from a dearth of quality resources!

How interested are inspectors going to be in my schemes of work? Should I be making any changes to them before the inspection?

Inspectors will be interested in schemes of work at your school, to a greater or lesser degree, depending on the main focus of the inspection. They will need to make sure that what goes on in the lessons they observe has a place in the grand scheme of things and that where pupils have been in terms of their learning relates to where they are going. There is no need to re-work these schemes (and there isn't time to anyway). As long as they are presented in a legible way, reflect what they should reflect and are followed by all who should follow them, all should be well.

In terms of assisting your inspectors in reporting positively, it would be a good idea to have some samples of work or lesson descriptions that were particularly inspiring. If you have these to hand in the event of an observation you can refer to them in the feedback session you receive. Likewise, if you have any specific plans for improvement in the future make sure that your inspector does not leave your classroom without being told about them.

Writing and re-working schemes of work takes a tremendous amount of effort and energy and should only be undertaken as part of your school's overall plan for development and not as a knee-jerk reaction to a likely inspection.

Find out more ...

- The Teacher Support Network will be able to guide in the event of inspection anxiety: www.teachersupport.info

CHAPTER 7

The experience of inspection

> The snow goose need not bathe to make itself white. Neither need you do anything but be yourself.
>
> Lao-tzu

Introduction

No two teachers will go through an inspection in the same way, but there will be certain features of the experience that are typically shared. Keep this in mind as you talk to colleagues when inspectors arrive at your school. It would be impossible to predict exactly what it will be like for you to experience an inspection but the following questions from teachers who have faced inspection before, and their associated answers, will help to show what might be a part of your experience. Above all else, view the experience of inspection from a position of empowerment; there's a lot that you can influence by your attitude and general approach and that influence isn't to be under-rated.

This chapter explores ideas around:

- the main features of inspection
- the focus of inspections
- observation of teachers
- how inspectors gather evidence
- meeting inspectors
- the pre-inspection days
- no-notice inspections

- meetings with inspectors
- duration of observations
- making an official complaint
- observation fears
- the involvement of pupils
- general preparation
- being observed with a teaching assistant
- feedback from inspectors
- misunderstanding and misrepresentations
- towards the end of inspection
- schools causing concern
- accepting inspectors' findings.

What are the main features of school inspection?

There are several main features of school inspection as described in the *Framework for Inspecting Schools in England from September 2005*, April 2008 edition (see below):

- inspections that are short and focused, taking no more than two days and drawing on interaction with a school's senior leadership team as well as using the school's self-evaluation as a starting point for the inspection;
- short notice of inspection so that inspectors get a better look at the school as it usually operates;
- inspections teams with few inspectors, many inspections being led by HMIs;
- a time period of three years between inspections, with those schools which are cause for concern being inspected more frequently;
- a strong emphasis on school improvement, drawing on a school's own self-evaluation, input from pupils, parents and others, and using this as the starting point for the inspection (this is why it is so essential for schools to stay up to date with their self-evaluation);
- common characteristics to inspection in schools;
- two categories of schools deemed to be causing concern: those requiring special measures and those requiring notice to improve.

You can find out more about these features of inspection from the Ofsted website (see below).

Does every feature of school life get covered by inspectors in the same amount of detail?

No, that simply isn't possible when they are only in schools for two days. Once your school has received notice of inspection, the lead inspector of the team that will be visiting your school will speak to your headteacher about the inspection, explaining that it will be very sharply focused (inspectors will have decided on the focus based on the pre-inspection data they have). While *everything* that goes on in your school feeds into its overall effectiveness as an institution, inspectors cannot subject it all to the same degree of scrutiny. Inspecting in this way, with a sharp focus, is thought to lead to greater school improvements and certainly helps to relieve the pressure on a school when inspectors visit.

Will every teacher in my school be observed?

No, not all teachers are observed. It's very unlikely that you will know in advance if you are going to be observed, but inspectors will certainly not be visiting every teacher in the school. This is because inspections are now much more sharply focused than they were in the past.

Inspectors do sometimes ask headteachers for (or rather, heads usually offer) suggestions of which teachers and classes to observe so that they see the range of quality in the school.

Inspectors are only in school for a very short period of time. How can they possibly get an accurate picture of what goes on here on a day-to-day basis?

Inspectors will have gathered a substantial amount of information about your school from all the self-evaluation that it does. This, and other data, will help inspectors to work out what focus they want the inspection to have. It is this self-evaluation that lies at the very heart of inspection, and offers inspectors 'crucial evidence' for their evaluations. Not everything can be inspected to the same degree of scrutiny so inspectors will carefully select what to focus on.

If there is anything that you definitely want inspectors to know about any aspect of your work in the school, tell them! That's perfectly acceptable. It may not feed into the actual report as they will be following their focus closely, but it will certainly feed into overall impressions.

Will we get a chance to meet inspectors before the inspection starts?

Inspectors don't visit schools in the few days between notice being given and the inspection actually starting. On the morning of the inspection, you will probably get the chance to meet inspectors briefly at least, so that you can put a face to a name and introduce them to the children should they visit your classroom.

Will I have any role to play in the pre-inspection days?

Part of the experience of inspection is the few days before inspectors arrive in school. These should be relatively calm and relaxed but invariably there's an air of anticipation (if not downright anxiety) about them. It's during these days that inspectors will be building relationships with your school's senior leadership team and agreeing the finer details of the arrangements for inspection. At this stage you should not be asked to produce any kind of documentation or paperwork for the inspection; inspectors will already be looking at all your school's self-evaluation data and other pre-inspection evidence. On the basis of all this evidence, inspectors will be determining the key issues for the inspection and discussing these with the school.

If my school is inspected without notice, does that mean that something is wrong?

HMCI does have the right to inspect a school without notice (the usual notice period for inspection is two clear working days) but this is only usually done when there are serious concerns about the well-being of pupils at the school. It certainly would indicate that something may be wrong if your school was inspected without notice.

Will I, as a teacher, be involved in any meetings with inspectors?

The chances are that you won't be directly involved in meeting with inspectors beyond the interactions you would expect if they observe a lesson of yours or watch an assembly or other part of school life. Your senior leadership team and governors will be meeting regularly with inspectors to discuss your school's self-evaluation and the issues that inspectors will be following through in inspection. If inspectors do want to have a meeting with you, this should be arranged as early as possible in the inspection proceedings. Usually it is only key staff who inspectors wish to hold meetings with.

Will I be told in advance whether I'm going to be observed teaching?

No, it would be extremely unusual to know in advance that you are going to be observed teaching. Inspectors will decide who they want to observe and will have a specific purpose for doing so.

If I am observed, how long will inspectors be in my room?

Inspectors don't have to observe full lessons and they are advised that generally, a half-hour visit to a classroom is appropriate. Observations do form an important part of the overall process but inspectors aim to gather the information they need from each observation relatively quickly and efficiently. There are occasions when shorter visits to classrooms are beneficial for a specific purpose and this will typically be around ten minutes, but there are no hard and fast rules.

If there are times when a teaching assistant takes your class either as a whole or in groups, inspectors may want to inspect him or her in action too.

Whatever inspectors decide to do regarding lesson observations, they should explain their rationale to your school. Inspectors will also usually offer headteachers the chance to conduct joint lesson observations (or scrutiny of work). Not only does this help schools to have a sense of shared ownership of the inspection and its subsequent evaluations, but it also gives headteachers guidance on making the kind of observations that inspectors undertake: all useful stuff in terms of general preparedness for inspection. These joint lesson observations tell inspectors a good deal about the quality of the leadership and management with regard to making judgements on teaching. The subsequent discussions that take place show how well heads take the opportunity to improve teaching and learning through their use of the evidence gathered in the observation. It goes without saying that after an observation, teachers should feel motivated, guided and fairly treated. During these joint observations, headteachers will be invited to grade the lesson against Ofsted's grade descriptions.

If a joint observation of one of your lessons takes place, the inspector should check with you first that you are happy with the arrangement rather than just assuming that you are. Heads will usually suggest that inspectors observe teachers who are not at the extremes of teaching in your school (for example, outstanding or inadequate). Those who are observed will usually be those who have been observed before and who are relatively confident with having other adults in the room while they teach. After a joint observation, the inspector will usually invite the headteacher to offer what they considered to be the overall strengths and weaknesses of the lesson. Inspectors will then offer their own views, and differences between the two judgements will be discussed. The inspector will then feed back to the head (or, on occasion, another senior leader who may be doing the observation) on the quality of their judgements and evidence. As a jointly observed teacher, your feedback would be given to you by the head, but observed by the inspector.

Joint observations are absolutely nothing to do with disciplinary proceedings or anything like that. They are simply a tool for helping inspectors to see another example of teaching and learning in the school and to understand how effectively heads and other senior leaders are supporting teachers in making improvements.

How do I make a complaint during an inspection?

Unfortunately there may be situations during an inspection which give you cause to complain. The usual route for doing this would be to speak to your headteacher as soon as the concerns arise. If your headteacher is part of the problem, then you may want to contact your union for confidential support and advice.

If you have cause to complain during an inspection, Ofsted strongly advises schools to raise their concerns with the lead inspector *as soon as they arise.* This is so that they may be resolved quickly while the inspection is taking place as it is generally harder to do this once the inspection is over. The key here is not to sit on any complaints and let them fester. Get them out in the open and dealt with as soon as possible.

If, having raised your concerns through the appropriate channels (usually your head, who will then speak to the lead inspector), you don't feel that they have been heard and dealt with as they should have been, you can contact the Ofsted helpline (see below).

Will inspectors want to talk directly to my pupils?

Inspectors do have to talk to pupils to gather evidence about the school to feed into their findings. Typically this can involve talking to year reps, the school council, or selected pupils during the course of a lesson observation. This is a bit of an unknown quantity but certainly isn't anything to worry about. The last thing you should try to do is script what young people should say or try unduly to influence which pupils speak to inspectors (and perhaps more importantly, which ones don't), unless, of course, inspectors ask you.

How can I prepare for being observed teaching by inspectors?

The short answer is that you can't really. Inspectors want to see how you usually teach, in all its day-to-day glory, not something that is exceptional and fundamentally unrepeatable because of the sheer amount of time it took to prepare. The best thing you can do is teach with confidence, skill and calm certainty that you are serving your pupils well. Don't aim for anything fancy (unless fancy is your usual style); just deliver a great lesson, with a clear beginning, middle and end and plenty of progression. Show that you are at home in your classroom and welcome any visiting guests with confidence. They are there to observe with an open mind and will not have made any judgements whatsoever before entering your room.

If I am observed, would it be for the whole lesson?

No, usually inspectors will observe a part of a lesson or session rather then all of it. If you are observed for part of a lesson or session, the inspector should let you know why this is.

I'm absolutely terrified that I'll 'corpse' in front of an inspector. How can I ensure I don't?

Be realistic! Have you ever done this during the course of your teaching career? What would happen if you did? Could you get out of the situation with a polite 'Sorry I've lost my thread. Where were we? Would anyone like to help? Remember to put your hands up'? Inspectors are human too and will be far more interested in how you deal with such an event than the fact that you corpsed in the first pace. Don't ever forget that there is no such thing as the perfect teacher. You're a human, not an automaton.

If you give the inspector a copy of the lesson plan you are using he or she will at least know where you are heading. It's a good idea to make sure that your lesson plans have the following features if possible:

- learning objectives
- timings (it doesn't matter if these are approximate)
- activities
- subject-specific language
- resources used
- the way teaching assistants will be deployed
- differentiation

- assessment for learning indicators
- where the lesson is heading next
- evaluation notes.

I have a fear that I'll reveal gaps in my knowledge in front of an inspector. How can I make sure that doesn't happen?

Although you will have prepared your lessons in fine detail, you can never know exactly what will arise in each one. There may well be questions from pupils that you are not entirely sure about, but again, remember that there is no such thing as the perfect, all-knowing teacher, and any inspectors that visit your classroom will be well aware of this. Once again, how you deal with this situation will be of greater interest than the fact that it has arisen at all. More often than not, honesty is the best policy. It is far better to admit what you do not know, than attempt to bluff and risk digging a deeper pit for yourself. As long as you arrange a time when you will be able to get back to the class or pupil with the correct answer, there is nothing wrong with saying that you don't know the correct answer to something. If you have the chance, tell any visiting inspectors that you intend to find out the answer and will recap on the question at the start of the next lesson. You could even invite him or her back to see what happens (although don't be surprised if they have seen enough).

What if I'm observed teaching one of my worst groups?

It does happen. If you know that you will be doing some particularly interesting work in a certain lesson it is perfectly acceptable to ask an inspector to witness it. The worst that can happen is that they say no. The important thing is that if you know that something is going to be good, give inspectors a chance to see it. If they can fit it into their schedule, they will. If they cannot, at least you have shown that you are embracing the spirit of the inspection and actively participating in the process, rather than being a passive recipient, and that is sure to go down well.

I work with a teaching assistant on some days. What's the best way to make sure that I maximise this situation if I am observed teaching?

Make sure that any adults who will be supporting you in your work receive lesson plans as soon as possible while the inspection is taking place (this is just good practice anyway). Aim to speak to them before each lesson or session to minimise the chances of confusion in front of an inspector. This isn't always possible but it does go towards helping things to run smoothly. Make sure that any support staff you work with are aware of the possibility of being questioned by inspectors. Don't be afraid to tell any observing inspectors how good your working relationship is and how it adds value to the work in your classroom. Much of this will be implicit in the way you interact but taking the time to put into words what you do together will ensure that you are both able to maximise the benefits to pupils when questioned by inspectors.

Encourage support staff to enter into a dialogue with inspectors should the opportunity arise: they don't have to wait until they are spoken to.

Finally, show inspectors any written guidance that you give to your support staff, especially if you recommend additional reading or resources on the work you are currently doing. Also, show any written methods you may use to enable your support staff to share information about pupils' progress and learning.

What if I can't manage the behaviour of pupils in a lesson that I'm observed teaching? If we get an inspection at the start of the academic year, I won't know all my pupils as well as I would if the inspection is later in the year and this seems unfair. Any top tips?

Even those teachers who rarely experience indiscipline and non-compliance in their classrooms have expressed this concern about inspection and it's perfectly natural. When you're dealing with growing and developing human beings you can't exactly demand compliance and predictability; that's not what young people are all about. Behaviour management is central to your work and many teachers achieve this through sheer force of character and personality. Therefore, it's easy to view any judgements made on your behaviour management skills as a reflection of your very essence. This seems to carry a whole lot more weight for many teachers than judgements made on other skills, hence the vicious cycle of anxiety.

If it is any consolation, most teachers report that pupils behave better than usual when an inspector is observing a lesson. In addition to this, any indiscipline, however minor, is an opportunity to show an inspector how you reinforce expected standards of behaviour and how you handle the 'miscreant' at the time. Don't worry about this fear. Even if the lesson is a disaster (extremely rare in Ofsted's experience) development needs will be flagged up and support should be forthcoming in the near future. Nothing is beyond repair. You may want to do some positive self-talk though, and affirm that behaviour in your classes is excellent.

If I am observed during the inspection can I expect any feedback from inspectors?

Absolutely: inspectors *must* offer teachers oral feedback about what they have seen. It might not always be possible to do this at the time, but inspectors should quickly arrange with you a time when it would be mutually convenient. This feedback must be crystal clear. Unless your lesson was utterly outstanding, which is always a possibility, inspectors will offer suggestions for improvements as well as telling you all about the strengths of the lesson. You should also be told the inspector's judgement on the overall quality of the lesson. Don't feel that you must simply listen and not speak: constructive dialogue between staff and inspectors is an essential part of the inspection process, so you should feel free to speak openly about what the inspector saw in your classroom and any other useful information that might inform his or her judgement.

Do keep in mind that there are several barriers to hearing feedback. These include:

- being preoccupied with the possible negatives;
- being preoccupied with the possible positives;
- feeling criticised or defensive;

- poor communication between you and the inspector;
- feeling that the inspector doesn't have the ability to comment on your work.

Each individual has a different capacity for hearing feedback, and self-knowledge will really help you to get the maximum benefit from the process. So many factors influence this, such as health, mood, energy levels and so on, that those offering feedback need to be well attuned and perceptive. Inspectors know that they must gain each teacher's acceptance and show sensitivity in the way they deal with teachers so if your communication skills are mutually effective, the feedback experience should be positive and constructive.

What if I am misunderstood or misrepresented in this inspection?

The chances of this happening are pretty remote but nevertheless some teachers have had this experience. If this happens during a verbal debriefing when inspectors are still in your school, the best way of dealing with this scenario is to talk to your headteacher who will be able to speak to the inspectors on your behalf. It's a good idea to keep a written record of what was said to you and what your objection is. If this doesn't resolve the situation then you may want to speak to your headteacher again and possibly your union too about making a formal complaint (see above). Don't be encouraged to let the matter drop if it is one that troubles you. It may seem like a hassle to correct what has happened, but it is important for your self-esteem and morale, and that's what your pupils need.

What will happen at the end of the two days that inspectors are in my school? Do they just leave and we have to wait for the report to arrive?

At the end of the inspection, the lead inspector will explain all the inspection findings to your school's senior leadership team and governors (at least the chair of governors). At this stage the report is subject to quality control and feedback and is only oral. The purpose of this exercise is to ensure that there are no unpleasant surprises when the written report arrives in your school. Inspectors will make clear any aspects which are judged to be inadequate or which they consider to be different from the school's self-evaluation. This feedback will also explain what the school needs to do to improve. It is important for those attending this meeting to understand clearly exactly what they are told and why the judgements have been made as they have. This feedback should, in turn, be fed back to other staff members and your headteacher will decide the best way in which to do this.

What if my school is deemed to be causing concern?

If your school is deemed to be causing concern, inspectors will categorise it either as requiring special measures or as requiring notice to improve. The *Framework for Inspecting Schools in England from September 2005*, April 2008 edition (see below), defines the former as:

> Schools which require special measures because they are failing to give learners an acceptable standard of education, and where the persons responsible for leading, managing or governing the school are not demonstrating the capacity to secure the necessary improvement.

Schools requiring notice to improve are defined as:

> Schools which require significant improvement because they are performing significantly less well than they might in all the circumstances in which they might reasonably be expected to perform. A school which is currently failing to provide an acceptable standard of education, but has the capacity to improve, will also be in this category.

HMCI has to personally authorise a report which states that the school requires special measures. If the draft inspection report on your school makes either of these judgements, your school's governing body will have five days to comment before the draft is finalised.

As far as you are concerned, as a teacher at the school, you simply wait for guidance from your senior leadership team on what happens next. Continue to teach to the best of your ability and be open to discussions about necessary development either for you personally or for the school as a whole. This is a potentially positive time for a school to bond and work together to bring about rapid yet lasting change and needn't be seen as a disaster in any way. Chapter 8 gives more detail about the aftermath of inspection. It's worth saying at this point that the vast majority of schools are not a cause for concern and will be given a grade 1, 2 or 3.

Will we as a school have to put up with all the findings of the inspectors?

While inspectors are in your school they will be meeting regularly to discuss their emerging findings. They will also be meeting with your headteacher and other members of your school's senior leadership team to discuss these emerging findings and offer the opportunity to provide further evidence. Yes, there is an opportunity to object if the inspection report doesn't accurately reflect the school, but every opportunity to show inspectors exactly what your school is achieving should be taken while they are still in your school.

Find out more …

- The *Framework for Inspecting Schools in England from September 2005*, April 2008 edition, can be downloaded from the Ofsted website: www.ofsted.gov.uk
- *Conducting the Inspection: Guidance for inspectors of schools* can be downloaded from the Ofsted website: www.ofsted.gov.uk
- The Ofsted helpline: 08456 40 40 40

CHAPTER 8

The aftermath of inspection

> Never go to excess, but let moderation be your guide.
>
> Cicero

Introduction

Breathing a massive sigh of relief may be the obvious reaction to the end of an inspection, and there's a lot to be said for putting it all behind you and moving on with your work and your life. But there is merit in taking some time to 'de-brief' on the inspection that has just taken place, and tie up any loose ends, whether emotional or practical, to ensure that maximum use is made of the experience. It's also important to celebrate your successes and to mark this important feature of your working life. Letting it slide by achieves neither.

This chapter explores ideas around:

- getting back to normal: restoring equilibrium
- inspection disappointment
- making complaints
- seeking feedback
- purposes of feedback
- causes of post-inspection stress
- combating post-inspection stress
- coping with 'snapshot' judgements

- dealing with perceptions of 'failure'
- the return of Ofsted for schools causing concern
- workplace bullying
- making progress from one level to the next
- finding relaxation time.

I'm finding it really hard to get back to normal after the inspection and I feel as though I'm risking my performance in the classroom. Do you have any tips for restoring equilibrium?

What is 'normal'? School life is so diverse and inspections and the associated aftermath really are a *normal* part of school life. You're not alone though; many schools report that life is not the same after an inspection and this is not necessarily a bad thing. As long as the experience has not left you gasping for breath, utterly deflated and bereft, the changes brought about may be refreshingly welcome.

These ideas may help you get back to some semblance of equilibrium after an inspection:

- Aim to include an on-going evaluation of your work as part of your definition of 'normal'. Do not go too long without requesting some form of observation by peers, leaders or managers.
- Focus on *identified* priorities, rather than on anything else. You do not need to storm ahead, all guns blazing; allow time for the dust to settle and for future directions to become clearer.
- Make a note of any procedural/organisational changes that you would like to make as a result of the inspection, however small they may be.
- Be sure to reinstate any events, treats or trips that may have been postponed until after the inspection.
- Avoid prolonged debate with pupils about the inspection now that it is over. Many heads like to address some of the issues raised by the inspection with pupils in some capacity and it is usually best not to add to this in your own classroom, if possible.

I was a little disappointed after reading the report on my school. I thought it would be more 'colourful' and reflective of the energy that my school has. Instead it seemed rather dry. Is that normal?

Inspection reports do tend to be fairly dry in that they have to be very succinct and evaluative. Inspectors are told to restrict the length of them to around 2,000 words for a secondary school and 1,500 for a primary school and within that there is a lot for them to report on. Reports should tell the 'story of the school' but are not often particularly creatively written. They mustn't be speculative or go anywhere to predict where the school may get to in the future: they relate to the here and now. The report is written primarily for the parents of children at the school but there is nothing to stop a school using the report as a basis and adding illustrative colour to it in a companion document for those who are interested to show a little more what the school is about.

I can't understand why my school didn't receive a higher overall grade. Why does that happen?

That is frustrating when that happens but if you haven't done so already, it might be a good idea to read the inspection report in full and carefully. Inspectors are supposed to explain in the report exactly why a particular grade is given and, importantly, wherever possible they should help the school in making improvements by explaining why a higher grade wasn't given (although they won't, or rather shouldn't, express judgements as recommendations). Look out for this as it should explain why your school received the overall grade it received.

Is it possible to make a formal complaint against Ofsted after an inspection?

Sadly it is sometimes necessary to lodge complaints as a result of an inspection even after all the necessary steps have been taken in raising concerns with the lead inspector and taking advice from the Ofsted helpline. If you find that any issues you have raised have not been satisfactorily dealt with then you can lodge a formal complaint. The timescale for doing this is at any stage *during* an inspection *or* up to 30 calendar days from the publication date of any report (or the end of the inspection if there isn't a report).

If you do decide to lodge a formal complaint this would normally be done with your headteacher and it is also advisable to seek the opinion and support of your union.

Formal complaints need to be made in writing and the contact details can be found below.

Once a formal complaint has been received by Ofsted, it will investigate it and respond within 20 working days. This response should cover all of your points of concern as well as details of how to take your complaint further (through an internal and independent review) if you are still not satisfied.

If you discuss the possibility of making a formal complaint with your headteacher, make sure that you are totally satisfied with the outcome of any such discussions. Never be tempted to put your concerns to one side for the sake of not 'making a fuss'. If in doubt, speak to your union for advice. *Do not let the matter drop if you have a genuine concern.* For what it's worth, only a very small percentage of inspections result in a formal complaint being made which does seem to indicate that lead inspectors deal with concerns effectively as and when they arise during the course of an inspection.

I sometimes feel as though I work in a feedback drought. Generally I get very little, but what would its purpose be in a school?

At its best, feedback can be a major source of positivity, allowing us to focus on what we have learnt and what we still have to develop. Both are valid and valuable lessons. You know what working life can be like without feedback; the chances are professional development is pretty haphazard in your school.

When you are listening to feedback being offered to you by anyone, keep in mind the purpose of the exercise:

- You should be given conclusions on your performance that have been reached through comparing your work against objective standards.
- Feedback should enable you to further develop positivity about your work (a common belief is 'that which is recognised and rewarded is repeated').
- Feedback should encourage you to move towards targets for improvement and help you to realise your full potential.

Feedback should not identify, or even highlight, major problem areas in your performance because there are other systems in schools for this purpose. It should never be a time of shock. If you come away from a feedback session remembering only the negatives, take care to think about the impact this is likely to be having on your daily life and work.

I feel as though we have been given very little feedback since the end of our inspection and I really feel out of the loop. What should I expect?

This is a relatively common complaint of teachers which is a shame as just a little more communication can alleviate this concern before it takes hold and starts damaging confidence. It's important not to fall into the trap of assuming that everyone else knows a whole lot more than you do. If you are feeling out of the loop, the chances are the rest of the staff at your school feel that way too.

The best way around this is to make a note of all your questions and arrange a time when you can speak to your line manager or headteacher. The chances are the post-inspection days have been so busy that information hasn't been disseminated quickly enough. It's difficult for headteachers to strike the right balance in this respect but it's safe to assume that the best thing for you to do for now is what you've always done. In time, you'll be informed of your school's development plans and should be consulted about what your precise role in those will be.

I want to avoid post-inspection stress. What seem to be the main causes of it?

Every teacher's experience of inspection is unique so there are no formulas for avoiding post-inspection stress. In addition, suffering post-inspection stress is by no means a foregone conclusion and the chances are you will sail through the experience and out the other side with no ill effects whatsoever. However, among those susceptible people who do suffer from lingering feelings of negative stress after the inspection has passed, there do appear to be several key reasons reported:

- **Change** There will almost certainly be some degree of change at your school as a result of the inspection even if the result is overwhelmingly positive. While this change may bring progress and improvement, it can be unsettling and demanding as adjustments must be made. The degree to which you respond to the requirement for change will impact your experience of post-inspection stress. The more open and flexible you are, the easier it will be. In addition, the more included you feel in the process of change (and this will depend on the way in which your school's senior leadership team decides to handle things) the more likely it is that it will not affect you adversely.
- **New job roles** The weeks following your inspection may see alterations to your job. Even if you welcome this, there may be an element of stress involved as you adjust to the new expectations.
- **Insufficient feedback on the next steps** There will be action to take in response to the inspection report, but this can be made difficult by inefficient communication between your school leadership team and other staff members.

The most important thing to remember is that your experience of post-inspection stress is ultimately down to the way in which you respond to these, and other, external factors. Aim not to allow them the power to overwhelm you.

The inspection at my school was several weeks ago but I still feel stressed about it. Why is that and what can I do about it?

It is ironic but it does seem that even when an inspection is over, related stresses can endure far longer than their useful purpose. A degree of what is known as positive stress is essential for our well-being: it motivates us to enjoy and achieve and to push ourselves beyond our current boundaries within a relatively safe context. Stress becomes a problem when it *prevents* us from enjoying and achieving: when it becomes a demotivating force, effectively making us less productive and more anxious about our performance than we might be. Sometimes it's very difficult to let go of feelings of negative stress and anxiety after the event for which we began experiencing those feelings has long passed. The reasons for this are often complex, and speaking to a trained counsellor can usually help in getting to the bottom of why you may be suffering extended inspection-related stress. The good news is that there is plenty you can do to help yourself back to a healthier experience of stress. These ideas will help:

- Aim to make a mental break now that the inspection is over. Do not take negative feelings associated with this experience forward into the future.
- Even if the outcome of the inspection has been beyond your wildest dreams (in a positive sense), do not be *surprised* by any feelings of negative stress. Good things can be stressful too (just think about how stressful it can be committing to a new partner, having a baby, moving house, and so on – these are all, ostensibly, positive experiences).
- Watch out for unexpected behaviour. Some teachers who have suffered through a stressful inspection, or from post-inspection stress, can find themselves behaving in unusual or unfamiliar ways. Do not give yourself a hard time over this, but do seek advice from your chosen healthcare provider if you are concerned.
- Your inner resilience has taken a knock if you are feeling the effects of negative stress after an inspection and you need to pay back

your 'overdraft'! Draw too heavily on your inner resources without replenishing them and the charges will be high. Be kind to yourself now; get as much rest as possible and adjust your expectations of yourself to take account of your feelings.
- Try not to feel contained and dominated by the whole experience. Stay connected with your purpose at work while you focus on the future.
- Resume your work–life balance (if it was knocked off-centre) as soon as possible after the inspection. If you felt, or still feel, extreme stress, this is unacceptable. It is advisable to see your chosen health-care provider with the intention of nurturing your mental and physical health. Try to convey to your leadership team and possibly to Ofsted itself (if a complaint is deemed necessary) the extent of your suffering.
- Remember that you are capable of learning that what once stressed you didn't kill you. The next time you experience inspection, the chances are the impact will be far less marked and potentially far more positive.

It's worth thinking about the idea that a 'tensionless' state is not a healthy one to head for. Many psychologists believe that we need to be striving for a meaningful goal rather than the banishing of all stress. In this respect, stress management is more about the creation of meaning through the tasks and goals that we set ourselves than it is about creating so-called 'tensionless' states. Think of the analogy of the decrepit arch: engineers *increase* the load on it, rather than decrease it, so that it is more firmly joined together.

Tension can be an amazingly useful development tool in our lives if we choose to experience it that way. To use this idea in connection with inspection-related stress, it can really help to look for the strengthening factors in your experience of inspection. In what ways has it led to a deeper reflection of your work in the classroom? Can you identify ways in which the experience has expanded your sense of meaning in your work? Given that inspection is a necessary dimension of the job of being a teacher, what positive links can you make between the experience and your practice? Being open to the possibilities of development is in the long run far less stressful than being closed to the good that each situation might present you with. And the great thing about this approach is that *you* are utterly in control; no one else can remove the good you decide to glean from the situation. That thought in itself should help to reduce any residual negative stress you may be experiencing.

The department I work in clearly came out badly in our recent inspection and I feel this is so unfair. Not all of us were observed, so how can they make judgements without seeing each one of us teach?

This is quite naturally very difficult to deal with. By its very nature, Ofsted can only provide a snapshot of what's going on in a school at any one time, but the data that it gathers and the conversations that inspectors have with your school's leadership team, its governors, other members of staff and pupils, not to mention the information it has from previous inspections, all feed into the inspection team's understanding of where your school is at. Although this system is inherently flawed, not even Ofsted itself would claim that it is perfect; it is what we have to work with.

There can be pockets of goodness, greatness and even excellence within departments or year groups deemed not to be performing as well as they might and that is worth acknowledging. The key to lifting you and your colleagues out of the disappointment of a lower than expected 'result' is to identify all those features that are working well and progressing as they should and apply some of those tools for success to the areas highlighted for development. Remember, nothing is *all* bad and there will invariably be strengths from which to borrow to bring the rest of the department up to scratch.

It's best if you can approach this with a sense of camaraderie. This isn't about competition, fault-finding or finger-pointing. Rather, it is about using each other's strengths to expand what's good and reduce what needs developing. Yes, it does seem harsh to be left feeling this way, but you can certainly be a very key part of the solution.

My school was recently inspected and found to be 'inadequate'. I'm finding this really hard to deal with. How can I keep it in perspective?

Words such as 'inadequate' and 'failing' are so difficult to deal with within the context of a school when teachers and other school staff are all about facilitating hope in learning. But as Mary Pickford said, 'What we call failure is not the falling down but the staying down.' These ideas should help you to see things as they truly are:

- If you are working in a school that has been deemed to be 'inadequate' in the standard of education it is offering, there is a need to focus on ways of bringing success, rather than failure, into the school's psyche. It can be difficult not to let the situation have a direct effect on your personal self-worth and self-esteem, but remember, you are just a part of a much bigger picture and cannot be held accountable alone.
- Ofsted has noticed that schools which are placed in special measures experience corporate emotions 'akin to grieving'. Anger and resentment are common stages in the grieving process, but when directed at the status of special measures, or even notice to improve, these emotions may do little to help move a school and its personnel forward, and a lot in attempting to apportion blame, which is *always* a futile exercise.
- It is not helpful to consider *yourself* as a failure or inadequate. It is the school in which you work which has been deemed to need improvement, and the work that you do there is dependent on so many different factors, not least the dynamics that exist between every member of staff. The quicker your school can actively launch into its programme of improvements, the quicker you will emerge successfully from notice to improve or special measures. At their most positive, these improvements will offer the potential for exciting regeneration that could be a thoroughly fulfilling experience.
- If you are finding it difficult to move away from the notion of 'failure', try speaking to the most positive members of staff to find out how and why they are viewing the situation as they are. Your

headteacher may also be able to offer some encouragement, as may your local authority. The Teacher Support Network can offer confidential counselling. You could also try focusing on an area of change that needs to be made and that can be achieved relatively easily. Congratulate yourself and others on *every* success!

- Do remember, too, that this is a temporary situation. Whatever the end result, your school will not be on notice to improve indefinitely.

When a school is deemed to be causing concern, does Ofsted return for another inspection quite quickly?

If a school is causing concern and placed in special measures, Ofsted will make a monitoring visit between four and six months after the inspection. Inspectors will make regular visits to monitor the school. These are typically termly, until the school is removed from special measures or re-inspected after two years (whichever of those comes first).

If a school is causing concern and given notice to improve, it receives a monitoring visit six to eight months after the inspection and another inspection 12–16 months after the inspection which gave it notice to improve. If the improvements made during that time have been satisfactory this inspection can remove the school from the 'causing concern' category.

I suspect that I may be being bullied at work and this has been going on since our inspection. Is there anything I can do about this?

There is always something that can be done about workplace bullying, however intractable the problem seems to be. Remember, it is illegal on several grounds and should not, under any circumstances, be tolerated or accepted.

The reason that bullying can take place after inspection is typically that school leaders feel pressured into making significant improvements too rapidly. Sometimes a scapegoat is sought and bullying begins. Thankfully this attitude is rare, but it can happen. If you feel that you are being bullied as a direct result of inspection, these ideas will help:

- Talk to a trusted friend or colleague about your experiences. Second opinions can help to re-establish perspective and may help you to decide whether or not to take action. You may also find that you are not alone in what is happening to you.
- Contact your union sooner rather than later. They will be very familiar with the phenomenon of workplace bullying and will almost certainly offer immediate advice as well as guidance on how to proceed to resolve the issue.
- Re-read your job description and any other information on teacher responsibilities in your school and in general.
- Document all communications between you and the person you suspect is bullying you, even relatively informal contacts. If you need to refer to previous conversations you will be pleased you have taken the time to record what has been said and when. Don't see this as unnecessarily paranoid; when you are working to resolve workplace bullying it is important to be prepared.
- Refute all unfair claims made against you.
- Monitor any changes in your performance at work which have occurred as a result of the bullying.
- Visit your GP even if your health does not appear to be suffering. It is sensible to formally record with your chosen healthcare provider what is happening to you at work and whom you consider to be responsible. Your GP should be able to offer stress-busting advice and will be a source of support should you need to take time off school.
- Read about assertiveness or attend an assertiveness course. If your professionalism is in question, you will need to be able to deal with the situation rationally and calmly. Professional counselling would also be a good idea. Contact your local authority to see if there is any available free of charge and you can also receive counselling from the Teacher Support Network (see below). Difficult as this may seem, try as much as possible not to allow the situation to permeate every aspect of your life.
- Ask for a copy of your school's policy on how it will deal with workplace bullying.
- Bullying destroys good teaching and you do not want to be faced with accusations of incompetence. Most unions have their own

guidelines on dealing with bullies at work available to members and non-members (although you may have to pay for literature from unions that you do not belong to).
- Read about workplace bullying so that you gain a background in this most damaging of practices.

Do remember that an Ofsted inspection is not sufficient evidence of incompetence, so however badly you think your work was reflected in the overall report, the outcome should not be used against you in any negative way. The whole point of inspection is to help facilitate improvements in the quality of education and care on offer to children and young people. This is achieved through support, not through bullying. Above all else, do not tolerate workplace bullying; it is illegal and *always* without justification.

There are several sources of support for the bullied teacher so never feel as though you have to struggle on alone – you don't. Support may come from:

- anyone who is not your bully
- your union
- Teacher Support Network
- your local authority
- books on dealing with bullying
- your GP or other healthcare provider
- family, friends and colleagues.

Remember, workplace bullying is relatively unusual, but if you think you may be a victim, it really is important to do something about it. Your physical and mental health can suffer by simply putting up with it.

I am delighted that my school was recognised as being 'good' and not 'satisfactory', but what happens now?

Being categorised as 'good' is a great achievement for a school and definitely cause for celebration. Take your time in acknowledging just what you have achieved as a team and how much your pupils are benefiting from your efforts. Be sure to take a good look through the inspection report, too, so that you know exactly what was thought about each aspect of your school's work. Aim to balance this with what your evaluations would be. Are there any surprises? There's no rush to do this; simply continuing as you were is perfectly acceptable for the time being and it's important to get back to your sense of equilibrium after an event such as inspection.

However, progress is the name of the Ofsted game and sooner or later your school will turn its attentions to how it can move from 'good' to 'outstanding'. This is the key question that all schools face – how to move from one level to the next. While your school will have collective ideas for how it is going to achieve this, it's likely that you will gain tremendously from looking into this for yourself too. One way of approaching this is to look at what it is that you do best of all in your job. What feature do you excel at? What are you passionate about? What makes this easy for you? In other words, why are you so good at it? What drives you? Make a note of your ideas. Now think about an area of your work that you might usefully develop. Next consider how you might use the skills and aptitudes that make you so good at the thing you excel at. How can you become passionate about it? What will assist you in moving towards being outstanding in it? Now that you have been through this process, be firm about not pursuing those activities which will not support you in your quest. You'll be amazed at how transferable our skills are across all the many features of life as a teacher, yet it's easy to get stuck in the belief that some things you can do well and with ease and other things you can't.

There is little available to individual teachers by way of support in making the transition from good to outstanding or any other transition, not least because it is *so* specific to the context in which you teach, as well as being dependent on the conscious choice and discipline of the individual to strive that far. That said, you may find it useful to explore some of the basic principles of stretching outcomes such as *Good to Great* by Jim Collins (see below); in particular look out for his work on the social sectors. He makes the very salient point that the path to greatness for teachers and so on does *not* lie in becoming more businesslike; most businesses, he says, are not in fact great.

In short, making the decision to move from 'good' to 'outstanding' is an important stage in your commitment to improvement. While the collective movement of your school is crucial, taking responsibility for creating so-called pockets of outstanding teaching and learning within *your* sphere of influence is the greatest contribution you can make. If every member of staff did this, and was utterly convinced by their ability to make a difference and feed into the progress of the school, there would be no limit to the transformations your school could make.

Successful as my school's recent inspection was, I know that I have to find quality relaxation time in each day because I cannot continue to work at the pace at which I have been working. What changes can I make?

You're absolutely right to focus on this need but you won't *find* time; you have to *make* time for relaxation. Teachers are creatures of habit: usually the work habit. For this reason many teachers must make a conscious *choice* to relax. This can be even harder than usual around inspection time and words such as 'should', 'ought to', 'got to' or 'have to' fill the minds of the conscientious. The autopilot steps in, the inner voice calling for rest and relaxation is silenced, and it becomes 'heads down for a crash landing'; for that is most certainly what will happen if quality relaxation time is not pursued with the same vigour that perfectionism in the classroom is.

The usual reasons for denying relaxation time are typically:

- I have to keep working because my competence depends on it;
- I have to keep working because if I stop I will never pick up the pace again;
- if I keep working I will make things easier for myself in the future, and then I will be able to take advantage of all my hard work;
- I have to keep working because it is lazy not to; relaxation is a waste of time;
- if I am not working, I am not achieving.

Are any of those statements familiar to you? Have you ever heard yourself using any of them? In reality, all of these reasons are nonsense and it is a perversion of reality to assume that you do not need to rest or do not have time to. Unless you allow yourself regularly to switch off from work, your performance will decline and your stress levels will soar; it is as simple as that. Relaxation is not an optional extra in your life but a vital necessity. Unless your body is able to relax, your responses to potential stressors will be far too quick, with physiological and psychological consequences.

Having a positive attitude towards relaxation is about giving yourself *permission.* Once you have done this, the most effective way of ensuring that you have time to relax on a regular basis is to commit to something that you find restful or relaxing. This might be some form of sport that you take part in each week, or a meditation or yoga class (with the added bonus of learning techniques that can be practised daily). Some schools even have organised relaxation therapies that staff can choose to take advantage of before leaving at the end of the day. If there is anything like this in your school, grab the opportunity with both hands.

If you do not have a slot in your life for 'active' relaxation, you are putting yourself at greater risk of succumbing to the ravages of unchecked stress. By investing in relaxation, your payback will be a greater ability to focus during the time you allocate to work, not to mention improved sleep quality and, in most cases, improved work performance and personal relationships too.

Find out more ...

- Formal complaints about Ofsted can be submitted in writing to enquiries@ofsted.gov.uk or to:
  The Complaints Manager
  Ofsted National Business Unit
  Royal Exchange Buildings
  St Ann's Square
  Manchester M2 7LA
- Teacher Support Network is accessible at www.teachersupport.info
- *Good to Great* by Jim Collins is accessible at www.jimcollins.com

CHAPTER 9

Using inspection for development

> Learning is not attained by chance, it must be sought for with ardor and attended to with diligence.
>
> Abigail Adams

Introduction

Without wishing to appear too dogmatic about this, there really is no point whatsoever in going through the process of inspection unless we use it as a professional and personal development tool. The great thing about taking this approach to inspection (and life in general) is that whatever happens, whatever our personal experience of the event may be, we can take something from it to help us transform some aspect of our professional or personal life. Using the experience of inspection in this way helps us to maximise its potential and promote change for the better, regardless of the outcome.

This chapter explores ideas around:

- being reflective and reflexive
- utilising feedback
- meeting professional development needs
- pacing change
- sustaining improvements
- being part of post-Ofsted improvements
- building confidence

- making changes
- enhancing your professional development 'mindset'
- balancing individual and institutional development
- making long-term use of the Ofsted experience
- evaluating the inspection experience
- keeping a professional learning journal
- building a professional development portfolio.

I want to develop my skills of reflection and reflexivity as a teacher, particularly in the light of our recent inspection. How can I use this experience to gain maximum professional learning?

As we've already seen in earlier chapters of this book, inspection can offer an unparalleled opportunity for professional and personal development if you choose to see it that way. A great starting point for this is to define what you mean by *reflection* and *reflexivity*. Useful ideas to consider are that reflection can involve careful mental consideration or concentration and reflexivity, which is a potentially deeper process, can involve a kind of'doubling' of the self so that we can both experience and observe what we are doing, what is going on for us and what we are thinking.

In all of this it helps to take your *self* into consideration. There should be a personalised link between you as the learner and the learning that you are seeking to integrate in your work, otherwise all you have is a series of disconnected and abstract experiences and no way of using them to further pupil progress and outcomes, not to mention your own satisfaction at work. Don't shy away from the impact that the *personal* can have. What did you learn as a person about your involvement in the inspection? To what extent is your self-knowledge enhanced? In what way do you envisage that feeding into your professional practice? The more consciously you adopt this kind of 'full-circle' thinking, the more you will gain from each learning experience in your work.

You may find it useful to keep a learning journal (see below) to enhance your skills of reflexion and reflection. While this may seem like another burden on your time, those who keep such a journal typically find it to be an incredibly powerful development tool with benefits that outweigh the sacrifices needed to keep it.

How can I make sure that I make the most of any feedback that I am given as a result of inspection?

Having been through the experience of an inspection and heard the feedback that inspectors and your headteacher and governors may have given you, it really is important to pull out of the information you have received the threads that can lead to future development and improvement. This is perhaps one of the most difficult aspects of the post-inspection phase as, understandably, the natural inclination is to get back to normal for a while. Facing new developments and even learning new competencies usually takes a level of enthusiasm that can be hard to locate among the recently inspected, if only because of their recent exertions.

For this reason it is essential to give yourself a break. You may be straight back at work immediately after an inspection and to throw in new goals for development from day one will prove to be self-destructive. Unless you are off to a new school which is about to be inspected, the chances are it will be a while at least before you have inspectors in your classroom again so you'll have plenty of time to digest everything you have learned and absorbed through the experience of inspection. In fact, there are some schools which advocate waiting as long as half a term before really analysing any feedback from inspection and using that to focus on any development needs. At least this way you have plenty of time to assimilate any information that the inspection has provided you with.

Here are some more ideas for making the most of the feedback you receive:

- Make sure that any feedback given does not contradict advice from other agencies or advisors, and openly discuss any discrepancies you may detect.
- Read the inspection report carefully and aim to be absolutely clear about the implications of each point made in it. If you need clarifi-

cation on anything, seek it from your line manager or headteacher. Do not leave room for any potential confusion. You should not be personally identifiable in the report but if you feel that you are and you have concerns about what has been written, talk to your headteacher and/or union about it.

- Consider carefully whether there is a need for professional or personal development training. Put your case forward as early as possible as resources may be limited.
- Think about whether or not there should be some changes made to the set-up in which you work. Are you working under unrealistic or incomparable pressures? Does the feedback that you have received indicate that your situation needs reviewing?
- Be prepared to push out the boundaries of success in the areas which have been highlighted as being in need of development. Pose challenging questions about your role and the improvements that are indicated. Use feedback to work *with* your school's team.
- Take time to appreciate all the successes that you and your school have achieved.
- Recognise that it is teachers, backed up by strong leadership, who are the agents of change. The feedback you receive can be used to help facilitate this, but inspection in itself cannot achieve it.
- Don't expect that the feedback you receive will feed into improvements in your practice overnight. This takes time and the notion of change and development, which is almost inevitable after an inspection (it's certainly desirable!), needs to sink down into the psyche of each and every one within your school community, teachers and learners alike.

Do not be contained or limited by any feedback you receive. However positive (or apparently negative) it may be, you can go beyond it and flourish further. Take the long view, welcome any changes that are necessary and celebrate what you do well.

Having been through an inspection I feel sure that I have some very specific professional development needs. What should my next move be?

First of all, make sure that you fully appreciate that there can be no such thing as 'mastery'. As soon as an individual or institution reaches a particular level of attainment, yet higher plains of competency come into view. However, it is the knowledge that there is no such thing as 'perfection' that puts schools and teachers in the best position for appropriate development. Being open to learning and to change is a true sign of success. If the feedback you have received is encouraging reflection, your purpose as a teacher will almost certainly be refined.

Talk to your school's professional learning leader or your headteacher about incorporating the development needs that you have identified as a result of the inspection into your professional development plan for the future. This is by far the most effective way of ensuring that the feedback you receive, combined with your own professional reflections, is utilised in the best way possible. Aim to be specific about what your new learning goals are and tie them in to teaching and learning in your classroom with your pupils. Do remember, too, that it can be the subtlest of changes in your work as a teacher which can bring about the most dramatic of improvements.

It can sometimes be the case that development needs, either of an individual or of a school, year group or subject area, are not picked up by an inspection and this can be quite frustrating for some teachers. Although it seems this is rare, knowing that there is a clear development need which isn't highlighted doesn't mean that the need no longer exists. In addition, what isn't highlighted can sometimes miss out on much needed resources to stimulate improvement. When identifying your own areas for personal and professional development don't feel that you have to be restricted by what the inspection may have highlighted. A bit of 'blue sky thinking' never did anyone any harm so incorporate those ideas into your discussions with your school's professional learning leader. Above all else, don't feel that you have to wait until your next performance management interview or professional review of progress before raising the possibility of targeting development.

One final word on this; do make sure that you are open to the possibility that what you have identified as a development need might not be deemed necessary by the powers that be in your school. If this is the case, and you are 'simply' lacking in confidence in a skill that you clearly possess, it may be that some in-house mentoring or coaching might be most appropriate. Sometimes it's helpful to let others be the judge of that, especially for the most conscientious teachers. And if you feel that your requests for development are not being heard, ask to speak to your headteacher about your concerns.

I've been through an inspection, but there is a clear expectation in my school to make all the necessary improvements virtually overnight! How can I keep a sensible perspective about this when I am not a part of the senior leadership team?

It is always a shame when schools react to inspection in this way. A far more effective response would be to take stock, allow feedback to be absorbed and to create an achievable and sustainable pace of development. Admittedly, it's important not to let improvement processes drift, without anchoring them to the current needs of the pupils and teachers at your school, but overly ambitious goals simply create negative stress.

A good way to deal with this as an individual (in recognition of the fact that you cannot, single-handedly, change the post-inspection culture in a school) is to break down what is expected of you into short-, medium- and long-term goals. Try to take everything on at once and burnout will result. Take things one step at a time and you're far more likely to be successful.

It's also a good idea to make sure that you fully understand *why* a particular change or development is indicated: this will avoid questioning of directives from on high. If you disagree with any decisions being made which impact your work in the classroom, do take the time to discuss your views with trusted colleagues and raise them with your line manager or headteacher as appropriate. Do not simply accept what happens if you have genuine concerns as this may stunt real growth for both you and your school.

The areas that I am responsible for did very well in our inspection and I fear that those areas that require improvement will now get all the resources thrown at them. What can I do to ensure that the standards I have managed to achieve are sustained and even improved now that inspectors have given them the thumbs up?

We tend to believe that the 'squeaky wheel gets the grease' – because those who shout loudest, or have the most obvious needs, tend to get the attention. This is such a common fear among teachers who are demonstrably effective and keen to maintain the standards they have already achieved.

Good leadership and management will ensure that resources are not only distributed according to need but also according to the need for all teachers to have the opportunity to develop their potential, whatever their starting point may be. If you feel that this is not the case in your school, speak to your headteacher about your concerns. It may also be a good idea to speak to your union rep about it too, and to document your concerns, especially if you believe that a lack of support for development is having a negative impact on your work.

What should you do if you think that you're part of the development plan for the post-Ofsted future without being consulted?

The short answer is that everyone is part of post-Ofsted development and everyone should be consulted so that they don't feel that development is being done *to* them rather than *with* them. The best approach when you feel that you are being 'dragged' along through change without being consulted is to think carefully about exactly what it is that your main concerns are, how they impact your work, and what resolution you would like to see. Then take these reflections to your line manager or head for discussion purposes. This isn't about behaving defensively or accusatorily, but rather it's about sitting down to discuss a mutually supportive way forward.

When you feel this way at work, the very worst thing you can do is nothing. That simply breeds resentment and in no way provides fertile ground for future development. Talk about it, sooner rather than later.

I found inspection to be a dreadful experience. My confidence is shattered and I want to give up teaching. What can I do?

Inspection is just one, relatively minor, aspect of life in a school. Yes, it is important, but there is so much more that happens in a school and so much more that you achieve through the course of your work. Don't hang everything on an inspection; they simply don't deserve that degree of power to disrupt your equilibrium to that extent.

Aim to determine why, exactly, you found the experience to be so demoralising. Be quite specific here; you're looking for identifiable reasons, not vague feelings. Write these down in as much detail as possible. Once you have your list of reasons for feeling this way, take each one in turn and write down an antidote. What will make you feel better about it? Do you need to talk to someone? Learn something? Do something differently? Make a complaint? Adjust your attitude? You will know what antidote will make you feel better about each point.

Once you have done this, write an action list. Aim to do at least one thing today, or in the very near future, towards easing your distress over this. Once you have done this, you'll see how quick and easy it can be to begin the process of transforming your response. That doesn't necessarily mean that you'll decide to stay in the profession, but it does mean that you are giving yourself a good chance of making an objective decision.

Remember that if you have been left reeling by inspection, something, somewhere along the line, went wrong. That isn't the intention behind inspection, and it isn't what inspectors are trained to do. For this reason it would be worth talking to the Teacher Support Network or to your union about what your next steps can be. They will also be able to offer confidential counselling which will help at this time. Above all else, aim to identify the ways in which this experience has given you a deeper self-awareness. This all helps towards developing your sense of resilience and will serve you well in the future. Make value in challenging situations; they have to teach you something, or they're simply not worth it.

I feel as though I have to change my working practices as a result of Ofsted. How should I approach this?

It's great if Ofsted has helped you to identify changes that you'd like to make in order to develop both professionally and personally. That's what it's all about and if we can use it to our advantage in this way, we're serving ourselves and our pupils well.

The best way to go about organising the changes you'd like to make is as follows:

- Write down (or record in some way) exactly what you have identified as needing to be changed.
- Think about what each change will give you and how each will impact on your work in the classroom. How will you and your pupils benefit from each change?
- Mark against each entry whether this change is essential or desired.
- Identify what support you might need in order to achieve the change. Would it entail resources such as time and/or money? Use evidence from the inspection to back up your reasons and desires for change.
- Identify against each change who might be in a position to help you.
- Now prioritise each change in order to create a personal action plan.

It is always worth discussing this kind of personal and professional development with your line manager, mentor or professional learning leader. Get support on board and it will be easier to reach where you want to be.

Inspection has shaken up my approach to professional development. I want to use it to enhance my 'development mindset'. What's the best approach?

The professional development 'mindset' is the greatest tool any teacher can have in the quest to improve in their work. More effective than money, it's the kind of attitude which helps you to gain from every situation and constantly consider how learning opportunities can feed back into your life and work. Successful and sustainable professional development is dependent on an attitude of mind and the fact that you have identified this puts you ahead of many.

Regardless of the external factors which may be impacting the professional development that you typically receive (such as the way that development is viewed in your school, the funds available to you, and the opportunities that present themselves to you), having a professional development mindset will ensure that you are able to over-ride difficulties and move on in your learning both despite and because of the resources available to you.

There is potential for professional development in every school day. It isn't confined to specific circumstances, reliant on pots of money or dependent on particular people. Development is an ongoing work in progress that can never be said to be completed during your working life. Therefore nurturing your professional development 'mindset' is not only about recognising opportunities for your own progress. It is also about recognising when you can contribute to the development of your colleagues too. We really are all learners, doers and teachers!

These ideas will help in your quest:

- Take a positive view of professional development. Everyone in every profession under the sun has to work towards furthering their skills and expertise and no one is immune.
- Be flexible in dealing with the unexpected or periods of uncertainty. This way you're more likely to glean maximum development potential from the situations that present themselves to you.
- Regardless of how ambitious or otherwise your goals are, you deserve quality professional development. Pursue this, and be aware that it can come in many forms.
- Once alert to the fact that professional development can happen every day, work at identifying just how much development your daily routine at school offers you.
- Be open at school about your desire for professional development. Make it known that you are fully committed to lifelong learning.

- Be completely ‘present’ at meetings. Ask all the questions you need to ask then and there. Not only will you gain from this approach but others will too.
- Ask about any aspect of your work that is not crystal clear. Make sure that you know why things are done in they way that they are and how this feeds into teaching and learning at school. Clear out any areas of confusion. This approach will engender an on-going connection with learning and professional development that will be fundamental to all aspects of your work.
- Don’t ever feel that you have to know precisely how to deal with every eventuality. You don’t, and thinking that you do (however competent you are told you are) can lead to missed opportunities for genuine professional learning. You don’t have to have all the answers all the time.
- If there’s ever the tiniest hint that you’re striving for perfection, drop the idea immediately: there is no such thing.
- Think about the ways that you communicate with other members of staff. Are there ways for you to nurture the development of others through your communication? Are you approachable? Are you willing to reveal your vulnerability in order to gain from the mutual benefits that can ensue?
- Be open about your willingness to share resources, ideas and information.
- Collaborate whenever possible. Two heads can usually make lighter work of a task than one. Avoid being a lone ranger – it rarely suits teachers!
- Consciously observe the professional differences that exist in your colleagues. Do this out of interest rather than judgement. Just how diverse is your staffroom?
- Never underestimate the benefits of networking with staff from other schools.
- Think about how you identify problems. Is it with possible solutions in mind or for the sake of locating the problem?
- Be patient with yourself. Professional development is not about cramming all your goals into a very short space of time. Your deadlines and ambitions need to be appropriate.

- Aim not to allow your quest for development to compromise your work–life balance.
- Ask for regular feedback. Be clear about what you want and who might provide it.
- Identify the ways in which the inspection experience has fed your development. What, exactly, did you learn about yourself, your work and the way your school operates? How can this feed into future improvements?

To explore the idea of professional development further, you may want to keep these questions in mind:

- How effective is your school at encouraging its teachers to keep professional development to the fore?
- How well equipped do you feel in identifying your development needs? How well are these needs met?
- Are you fully aware of your motivations when it comes to professional development?
- What is it that you do well? What can you contribute to the learning of others?

Going through the inspection has made me appreciate more fully the tension between institutional and individual development. An inspection focuses everyone's mind on what the school as a whole needs to do but how can we prevent the individual from being lost in all this?

This is a common concern but it needn't be an issue. It could be argued that all professional development that individual teachers achieve cannot fail to have an impact on the overall development of the school in which they work and likewise, all development undertaken to meet the needs of the school cannot fail to have a impact on the individual.

In an ideal world, the ambitions and targets of the individual would be perfectly matched to the perceived needs of the school but that doesn't always happen so a balance needs to be sought between these two potentially conflicting aims. Being totally clear about the direction in which you would like to move in your professional and personal development is a useful first step. If you know where you want to go, why you have chosen this development path and how it will fit into your work in the school, you are in the best position to be able to pursue it. It is even better if you can link it in, somehow, directly with the Ofsted report. It is also a good idea to research any funding which might support your plans. Talk to your school's professional learning leader and take a good look at the Training and Development Agency for Schools website to see what is available.

Steering clear of any potential tensions between individual and institutional development is largely about communication. Being realistic about your development needs, and knowledgeable about your school's plans for development, will help to ensure that the two dovetail rather than clash, and this is the ideal aim.

I've just been through an inspection in one school, but I'm leaving to pursue my career in another school. Was the last inspection irrelevant to me or is there something I can take from it to put to use in my new school?

Inspection of one form or another is a fact of life in just about every type of school. Each experience of inspection, while specifically targeted at the school in question, will offer generic development which will serve you well in just about every setting you work in. Think about these points:

- You now know what impact the inspection had on you personally: what your response to the situation was, how you coped, what enduring effect it had. This is incredibly useful information for the next inspection, wherever it is that you experience it.
- You have experience of general preparedness for inspection (or not, as the case may be) and can take that with you, making a note of what you might do differently in the future. Remember, little or no notice of inspection is here for the foreseeable future so long-term preparedness is the way to go.

- You may have experience of being observed in your classroom and may also want to maintain that through taking part in on-going peer observations for the benefit of your continued professional development.
- You have crucially valuable experience of the post-inspection phase, the impact this can have on a school and the way in which the impetus for development can be handled.
- You are now far more familiar with the nitty-gritty of inspection, its processes and features, and fear of the unknown won't affect you.
- You may have experience of the degree to which you can challenge inspectors on their findings, either directly, or through your headteacher.
- You have lived through the inevitable adjustments to your working practices which naturally occur as a result of inspection.
- Your experiences of a recent inspection are likely to be of interest to those at your new school if an imminent inspection is likely there.

I intend to remain in the teaching profession for the foreseeable future. How can I evaluate my recent experiences of inspection so that I can use my reflections to my benefit in the future? After all, it seems inspection is here to stay!

Your school will probably want to carry out some form of evaluation on how well you all coped with the inspection (after all, there cannot be a reflective practitioner in the land who does not strive for increasingly better ways of doing things). The main aims of such processes are to define what went well and what should perhaps be done differently next time.

For your part in this evaluation process, these ideas may help:

- Keep a note of any aspect of this inspection which has caused you anxiety. Be as specific as possible and record what helped you and what hindered you. Can you identify what the source of the anxiety might have been? Was it pressure you put on yourself or was it imposed on you by others? Aim to re-read what you write the next time you receive notice of an inspection as it may help you to avoid a recurrence. It's also helpful to read through any such notes periodically to see how you have developed in your approach to potential stressors at work. Think of this exercise as advice to your future self.

- Consider what knowledge of yourself you have gained through the inspection. What personal development have you experienced? Has it taught you anything about the way in which you handle such situations? Has it extended your self-understanding?
- Take a moment or two to reflect on the school in which you work, now that it is in its post-inspection phase. Are you in an environment where you can flourish? Are you and the school 'compatible'?
- What about your contribution to the school? Are you a key member of staff who could offer more? Can you see your relative position more clearly? Has an official hierarchy developed or been exploded as a result of the inspection?
- Were there any aspects of observation and scrutiny that concerned you? What would make you feel more comfortable about this process?

One very useful action to take in the immediate aftermath of an inspection is to take some time to reflect on exactly how you experienced the process. Was it stressful in any way? What contributed to that feeling? How did you attempt to alleviate that? What helped and what hindered? How would you do things differently in the future?

Do remember that as a teacher (and as an individual) you amount to so much more than any judgement of your performance. In fact inspection has never been intended to *define* or identify you, but merely to take a snapshot of where you are at present, not where you will be in a term's or a year's time.

I'm interested in starting to keep a professional learning journal, not necessarily for use every day, or solely as a result of the inspection, but I like the way that the inspection has provided a focal point in my career to date and I'd like to be more mindful of where I'm going from here. Any ideas on how to do this in such a way that I'm likely to keep it up?

Writing down your thoughts and reflections can be an excellent way of developing your skills as a teacher and of appreciating a sense of movement in your professional and personal development. There are various forms and styles of writing for journal keeping, and in turn, these vary in the use and value that they can have in your teaching career.

Those who keep professional learning journals often say that it helps to distinguish (before putting pen to paper) between writing intended for personal use only, and that which may form part of a professional development portfolio. This can help to avoid the need for re-writing at a future date and can also keep you focused on what is meant for you and what you would be prepared to share with others.

The field related to the use of writing (creative or otherwise – in fact some schools of thought argue that *all* writing can be deemed creative writing) is developing fast. Writing is increasingly being advocated as a professional and therapeutic tool for discovering more about oneself and is successfully being used in a variety of contexts such as schools, prisons and hospitals.

It is useful to view such a professional learning journal as being for your eyes only, unless you have a specific reason not to – for example, undertaking a course which requires submission of a journal for assessment purposes. Otherwise, aim to keep it private so that you are able to be as candid as possible. These ideas will help:

- Expect it to take a while to get into. You might make your first entry and then leave it for a week or more before attempting another but this is usual. There will come a time when you regularly turn to your journal and the more you do this, the more valuable the process becomes: but certainly don't force the issue. Your commitment to a learning journal is likely to emerge in time and that's fine.

- Seek to push your self-understanding through your journal. It isn't a place to be complacent about your work at school. Rather it's a safe space in which to nudge yourself towards greater understanding and a wider perspective, as you explore key themes of your day with empathy towards yourself and others.
- It may sound flippant, but organise *how* you are going to record your entries. Whether online or on paper, or even recorded to a CD, make sure that it is a method that suits you and is sustainable. While we may well live in the truly technological age, it's hard to beat a nice, easily accessible notebook and pen.
- Don't think that you have to structure your journal – you don't. You can add notes to it as and when the need arises and they don't have to link, necessarily, to previous entries. To get best use from this you might want to seek to make meaning of what you have written, but this process may happen some time after the original reflection is done.
- Aim to use this learning journal, also, as a chronological record of significant events in your career, such as professional development courses and events, and inspection.
- When you are in a hurry, but still want to make an entry, consider the use of single words in conveying a sense of the day or of a particular event or challenge. Sometimes being able to distil in this way is incredibly powerful and effective as a development tool.
- You may want to experiment with a 'double entry' system. This means writing a factual account of whatever you want to reflect on, and then a reflective account. Use this reflection to work out how you might feed back into your work a more enlightened approach.
- If you want to be more structured about this, you may want to consider doing specific writing exercises every day, or at regular intervals such as weekly or monthly. Aim to answer key questions related to your work as a teacher (for example, what went well today, what would I change, what development needs have emerged, what progress can I sense in myself, and so on).
- Consider writing an autobiography, using vignettes of your life as a teacher, almost like a written photograph album.
- Start to consider using what you write in your learning journal to sit alongside other aspects of your professional development.

For example, this journal will be particularly useful to accompany studies on a work-related higher education course.

- Think about pulling out of the greater mass of your learning journal particularly poignant vignettes of reflective and reflexive writing.

Having been through an inspection I can now see how valuable it is to build up a professional development portfolio. What's the best way of going about this?

There are very few better ways of seeing at a glance just how much progress you have made and what you have achieved throughout your working life than by maintaining a professional development portfolio. Your experiences of inspection can feed into this too and provide you with an excellent record of how you got to where you are now.

Part of being a reflective practitioner is the very practical job of keeping documentary evidence of your achievements, areas of expertise and learning priorities. This basically means making sure that:

- your CV is as up to date as possible;
- you have an ongoing list of skills you would include in your supporting statement (don't ever go as far as actually writing a supporting statement – this has to be done when you are actually applying for a job so that you can match it precisely to the person specification);
- you keep your professional development portfolio up to date.

If you're setting about creating a development portfolio from scratch, remember, this is about gathering together tangible evidence of your achievements and progress. These ideas will help:

- An A3 folder is a good size to go for and these can be bought from art shops, stationers and office suppliers. This size allows you to include photo displays and examples of children's work, but do this only if relevant to your portfolio.
- Consider including an electronic version of your development portfolio too. A memory stick containing, for example, relevant PowerPoint

presentations and electronic versions, where possible, of the printed matter can be useful. This could also include your school's latest Ofsted report.
- Aim to cover the breadth of experience that you have, but remember that relevance is key. This isn't about throwing everything you've got at it! Be selective.
- Devise a CV and aim to keep it up to date. This is an excellent way of organising relevant information about yourself. Don't be tempted to just add to your CV when you have something else to include. Instead it's worth doing a complete revision so that it remains as up to date and relevant as possible.
- Don't shy away from including examples of learning which has not been as effective as you hoped. This is a chance to show what you gain from adverse experiences and that you are committed to professional development.
- Keep the contents of your portfolio organised so that they are easy to retrieve for the purposes of discussion.

You might also want to keep a running list of all the professional development courses you complete as well as all the activities and exercises you undertake as part of your work which impact your development, for example, participation in performance management and peer mentoring. It helps to include just enough information to prompt you when you need to speak or write about what you have achieved. Aim to link your learning with progress in your pupils.

It can also be a good idea to organise your professional development portfolio around the national priorities for CPD. At the time of writing these are: pedagogy (behaviour management, subject knowledge, supporting curriculum change), personalisation (equality and diversity, special educational needs and disability) and people (working with other professionals, school leadership). You can find out more about this, and other current features of CPD for teachers, from the Training and Development Agency for Schools website (see below). It can be time-consuming, but if you set aside time regularly to keep on top of your portfolio, you will definitely reap the rewards.

Find out more ...

- The Training and Development Agency for Schools: www.tda.gov.uk
- For guidance on writing with a view to enhancing personal development try *Writing: Self and Reflexivity* by Celia Hunt and Fiona Sampson, Palgrave, 2005, ISBN 1403918775
- For information on reflective professional development practices try *Reflection in Learning and Professional Development: Theory and Practice* by Jennifer A. Moon, Kogan Page, 2000, ISBN 074943452X

Index